MONETARY, FISCAL AND TRADE POLICIES

TRADE LIBERALIZATION

GLOBAL POLICIES, BENEFITS AND ECONOMIC RISKS

MONETARY, FISCAL AND TRADE POLICIES

Additional books in this series can be found on Nova's website under the Series tab.

Additional e-books in this series can be found on Nova's website under the e-book tab.

MONETARY, FISCAL AND TRADE POLICIES

TRADE LIBERALIZATION

GLOBAL POLICIES, BENEFITS AND ECONOMIC RISKS

PAULINE SANTOS
EDITOR

nova publishers
New York

Library of Congress Cataloging-in-Publication Data

Names: Santos, Pauline, editor.
Title: Trade liberalization : global policies, benefits and economic risks/
Pauline Santos, [editor].
Description: Hauppauge, New York : Nova Science Publishers, Inc., [2015] |
Series: Monetary, fiscal and trade policies | Includes bibliographical
references and index.
Identifiers: LCCN 2015037931 | ISBN 9781634838672 (hardcover)
Subjects: LCSH: Free trade. | Commercial policy.
Classification: LCC HF1713 .T69495 2015 | DDC 382/.71--dc23 LC record available at http://lccn.loc.gov/2015037931

Published by Nova Science Publishers, Inc. † New York

CONTENTS

PREFACE

This book provides research on the global policies, benefits and economic risks of trade liberalization. The purpose of the first chapter is to examine the role of agricultural trade in promoting global food security. The second chapter discusses corporate social responsibility, trade liberalization and global welfare. Chapter three sheds light on the role of the state in determining international competitiveness of agricultural commodities and the pattern of agricultural trade. The final chapter of this book studies the impact of trade liberalization on the Australian manufacturing sector.

Chapter 1 – The purpose of the chapter is to examine the role of agricultural trade in promoting global food security. Consistent with the literature on agricultural trade, the authors believe that agricultural trade liberalization (removing all trade barriers including domestic policies) would be a powerful instrument in the long run for promoting global food security, potentially boosting agricultural growth in Sub-Saharan Africa and South Asia, which represent the regions most vulnerable to food insecurity. Indeed, it would be a much more effective strategy than any other efforts at the global level such as increasing food aids, foreign aids, foreign direct investment, or preferential treatment. However, as evidenced through the Doha Round, trade liberalization in agriculture is next to impossible in the real world for some political and other inherent reasons that make it practically infeasible to have free trade in agriculture. The authors contend then that the next best strategy is to remedy the uneven playing field in agricultural trade that has been shaped during the postwar period by agricultural protection in developed countries and agricultural taxes in the developing world and reinforced by the current WTO trade rules.

Chapter 2 – In an international duopolistic market, the consumer-oriented CSR initiatives will make the domestic government lower the tariff rate if the weight is relatively high in both cases of dual CSR and unilateral CSR by the foreign firm; however, the government will raise the tariff rate if the weight is relatively high in the case of unilateral CSR by the domestic firm. Furthermore, the consumer-oriented CSR initiative of both firms is the dominant strategy if the CSR cost is sufficiently low. More importantly, the consumer-oriented CSR initiative of both firms is the global social welfare optimum if the CSR cost is sufficiently low coupled with trade liberalization.

Chapter 3 – This chapter attempts to shed light on the role of the state in determining international competitiveness of agricultural commodities (unprocessed) and the pattern of agricultural trade. Farmers are neither the ones who make decisions whether or not to enter international markets nor are the ones who invest in R&D and attempt to develop new technologies with the goal of enhancing international competitiveness. Liberalizing trade is likely to send signals first to trading corporations, grain handlers, and governments and transmitted to farmers indirectly. Freer trade would initiate the process of specialization of production across the world, generating benefits in terms of greater production and lower prices, but offering little additional incentive for individual farm producers to reduce costs or adopt new technologies for the purpose of enhancing export opportunities (hence, lacking the creative destruction processes like in the manufacturing sector in which firm level strategies would determine international competitiveness). However, states may compete with each other to expand their exports or to decrease their dependence on food imports with strategic investments in agricultural infrastructure. The point is that state level strategies will determine the pattern of agricultural trade in the long run. The implication for low-income/food insecure developing countries is that the state should play a proactive role in advancing agricultural development and making investment decisions for building agricultural production capacity (through public investments in R&D and extension services) and constructing/fostering the markets for agricultural inputs (credits, risks, information, transportation, managerial).

Chapter 4 – Trade liberalization has been at the epicentre of the restructuring of manufacturing exports from the simply transformed to the elaborately transformed manufacturing products which are more competitive on the international market. This has sharpened the export focus of the Australian manufacturing sector thereby providing a platform for stronger output and employment growth. However, manufacturing products as a proportion of total exports has exhibited a downward trend which has led to the persistence of a narrow primary product export base. This in turn has resulted in sustained terms of trade-induced income losses and fluctuations in export revenue and hence output and employment growth.

In: Trade Liberalization
Editor: Pauline Santos

ISBN: 978-1-63483-867-2

Chapter 1

WHAT IS THE ROLE OF AGRICULTURAL TRADE IN PROMOTING GLOBAL FOOD SECURITY?

Wanki Moon[1,*], Gabriel Pino[2] and Hyeon Joon Shin[3]
[1]Department of Agribusiness Economics,
Southern Illinois University, Carbondale, IL, US
[2]Facultad de Economía y Negocios, Universidad de Talca, Talca, Chile
[3]Falls School of Business, Anderson University, Anderson, IN, US

ABSTRACT

The purpose of the chapter is to examine the role of agricultural trade in promoting global food security. Consistent with the literature on agricultural trade, we believe that agricultural trade liberalization (removing all trade barriers including domestic policies) would be a powerful instrument in the long run for promoting global food security, potentially boosting agricultural growth in Sub-Saharan Africa and South Asia, which represent the regions most vulnerable to food insecurity. Indeed, it would be a much more effective strategy than any other efforts at the global level such as increasing food aids, foreign aids, foreign direct investment, or preferential treatment. However, as evidenced through the Doha Round, trade liberalization in agriculture is next to

* Wanki Moon: Department of Agribusiness Economics, Southern Illinois University, Carbondale, IL 62901. E-mail: wmoon@siu.edu.

impossible in the real world for some political and other inherent reasons that make it practically infeasible to have free trade in agriculture. We contend then that the next best strategy is to remedy the uneven playing field in agricultural trade that has been shaped during the postwar period by agricultural protection in developed countries and agricultural taxes in the developing world and reinforced by the current WTO trade rules.

Keywords: agricultural trade, global food security, trade liberalization, agricultural protection

INTRODUCTION

Despite more than seven decades of "development" and "globalization" processes since the end of the Second World War, food systems have failed to deliver food security at the global level and face increasingly uncertain future in their capacity to expand production. There are nearly one billion people suffering from chronic lack of access to food and another billion suffering from micronutrient deficiencies. While the overall number of food insecure people has been declining over the last decades thanks to the remarkable economic performances in China and India, the number of such people has increased in Sub-Saharan Africa and South Asia. Hence, the global food insecurity is a problem of the retardation of agricultural and economic development in the two regions. Further, apart from the regional disparity in accessing food, the global food system needs to increase food production by 70 percent to surmount expected food shortages at the global scale in association with population growth to 9 billion by 2050, rapidly expanding middle class, urbanization, and subsequent increases in meat demand in the developing world (FAO 2010, Godfray et al. 2010, Foresight 2011). The challenge is to achieve the increase in food production under the constraints of warming planet and growing water scarcity.

The purpose of the chapter is to examine the role of agricultural trade in coping with the global food insecurity problem. The orthodox theory of trade contends that free trade would stimulate economic growth and consumers' demand for environmental quality, compel governments to tighten regulations, and facilitate improvements in environmental quality.

There are other theories, however, countering the orthodox theory ranging from the infant industry protection argument in the 19th century to the more recent new/strategic trade theory to ecological economic thinking as reflected in the concepts such as the environmental carrying capacity as a limit to economic growth, unequal ecological exchange (the North is transferring environmental damages/costs to the South), and persistent underpricing of natural capital stock and consequent overuse/degradations. Defying the conceptualization of the virtuous effects of free trade on economic growth and the environment, these counter-theories underline the substantive role the state has to play in managing trade to promote economic growth and achieve economic development in an environmentally sustainable way.

In congruence with the mainstream theory of free trade, the World Trade Organization (WTO) has been making persistent efforts to reduce trade barriers in agriculture over the last decades. Proponents for such WTO efforts contend that there are two particularly important benefits of liberalizing global trade in agriculture. First, freer trade in agriculture would contribute to growing the global economy by fostering specialization of production across the world. Research estimates that there would be substantial increases in national incomes and welfare associated with trade liberalization for all countries involved (Anderson and Martin 2005, Hertel and Keeney 2006, McCalla 2003). In particular, Laborde, Martin and van der Mensbrugghe (2011) show that about two-thirds of the economic costs of trade barriers at the global level are associated with distortions in the agricultural sector and nearly 70 percent of the potential benefits from liberalizing global trade would come from reforms in agricultural trade, given that there is not much distortion to be corrected in the manufacturing sector and therefore not much to be gained from further liberalization, it is important to liberalize agricultural trade as a way of stimulating and growing the global economy. Second, research indicates that full liberalization of trade in agriculture would confer disproportionately greater benefits to the developing world because it would have access to the agricultural markets in developed countries, thereby helping its agricultural sector to grow; and agricultural growth is most effective in reducing poverty given that the majority of people living with less than a dollar per day resides in rural areas (Barichello, McCalla and Valdes 2003, Anderson and Martin 2005). Anderson (2005) estimates that the gains to the developing world would be greater than the size ($60 billion per year) of official development assistance (ODA) and the size ($150 billion per year) of foreign direct investment (FDI) from OECD to developing countries. The studies above suggest that even unilateral liberalization by the developing world without corresponding liberalization from the developed world would generate significant benefits to the developing world.

Launched in 2001 in Doha, Quatar, the Doha Development Round has lasted about 15 years now without reaching a multilateral agreement despite the solid foundation laid by the Uruguay Round Agreement on Agriculture (URAA) in 1994. There are explanations for the failure of the Doha Round that are related to the process of reaching a multilateral agreement within the WTO such as the large number of member countries and mediaeval decision-making procedure, the changing geopolitical environment (the rise of BRICS as a major negotiating power), and the Single Undertaking (indicating that agreements much be reached simultaneously for all areas including agriculture, manufacturing, services and others). Yet, more substantive explanation is the discords of member countries on what exceptions (e.g., nontrade concerns; sensitive and special products; special safeguard provisions against import surges) should be permitted to what extent (Collier 2006, Martin and Messerlin 2007). Underlying such disagreements is the diversity of the innate positions various regions/countries across the world have taken on agricultural trade during the Doha negotiations. For example, the Cairns group (e.g., Brazil, Indonesia, Australia) advocate outright liberalization of agricultural trade consistent with their natural comparative advantages in the agricultural sector; the EU and other industrialized countries use the concept of "multifunctional agriculture" to maintain the flexibility to choose policy instruments appropriate for their national or agricultural sector's needs; the US advocates for agricultural trade liberalization and put forth proposals of bold cuts in its farm subsidies but do not act unilaterally (it will act only if the EU is willing to match such proposals); developing and least developed countries want to maintain the flexibility in choosing policy instruments in order to adequately address their food security concerns.

Such diverse positions of WTO member countries in the Doha Round reflect conflicting interests across countries/regions that originate from non-uniform roles of agriculture for countries at differential developmental stages. For middle-income countries, the agricultural sector plays a critically important role for sustaining economic growth; it is needed for tropical countries to strike a balance between agricultural expansion and preservation of rainforests for the global community's fight to reduce carbon emissions; for least developed and developing countries, the agricultural sector is indispensable for kicking off the process of economic development/growth and promoting food security, thereby reducing poverty/hunger; for developed countries, the agricultural sector is vitally important for producing a variety of nonmarket goods and services (ecosystem services, water purification, nutrient recycling, farm amenities, vitality of rural economics); and for developed net food-importing countries, the agricultural sector is important for providing a minimum level of domestic production needed in cases of international crises (e.g., war; natural disasters). Given the cross-country diversity in the roles of agriculture, it appears inappropriate to apply uniform rules to all countries.

This chapter is organized as follows. The next section describes what it means by global food security. The third section analyzes the pattern of agricultural trade and shows that the current pattern of agricultural trade is shaped by both natural comparative advantages and policy-induced advantages. The fourth section sketches out the short and long-run effects of removing all barriers to trade and domestic subsidies on the pattern of agricultural trade. The fifth section analyzes the linkage between agricultural trade liberalization and global food security. It emphasizes the important role of the state in determining the long-term effect of agricultural trade liberalization on ameliorating global food insecurity. The last section provides some suggestions for trade rules that would be conducive to promoting global food security.

THE MEANINGS OF GLOBAL FOOD SECURITY

The notion of global food security has two distinctive aspects. First, it connotes the capacity of the global food system to produce food sufficient enough to feed all people living on this planet in a sustainable manner. This definition of global food security emphasizes the supply side capacity to produce food given environmental and natural resources constraints (e.g., arable land, water shortages, soil/land degradations, carbon emissions). Second, it refers to the ability of each person on this planet to have access to nutritious food under any conditions and underlines the importance of effective distribution system within a country and across countries, more consistent with Amartya Sen's Entitlement Approach to food security. While the first type of global food security is a grave challenge that our world should cooperate to address, the more urgent problem is the second type of global food security. That is, significant portions of people in some regions of the world (particularly Sub-Saharan African and South Asia) live with less than a dollar per day, preventing them from accessing sufficient amounts of food. The majority of them live in rural areas and the agricultural productivity is not high enough to secure sufficient quantities for domestic consumption or to earn sufficient amount of income from the sales of their agricultural products.

This chapter has immediate connections with both definitions. That is, trade rules on agriculture can have significant effects on the capacity of the global food system to produce food *via* various channels such as specialization and technological advances/transfers, land use patterns, production efficiency (both technological and organizational), and sustainability of natural resources (e.g., water; soil; land degradation; carbon emissions; biodiversity). Likewise, trade rules on agriculture can have profound effects on food distribution across regions/countries. We would normally conceptualize that freer trade would be more conducive to more efficient food distribution across countries because countries would have better access to the world agricultural commodity markets. However, the distribution issue may not be that straightforward and a number of questions may arise. What if the global commodity markets are dominated by a few large multinational trading corporations and international prices significantly diverge from competitive prices? What if net food-importing countries do not have the financial means to procure food in international markets? What if natural disasters (more likely in this climate change era) hit a region of major agricultural exporting countries under a very specialized international agricultural production system? What if food-importing developing or least developed countries cannot have economic growth/development without first undergoing agricultural growth and development? With an eye on these questions, this chapter explores how agricultural trade is linked to global food security.

AGRICULTURAL PROTECTIONISM AND THE PATTERN OF AGRICULTURAL TRADE

The pattern of agricultural trade would be determined by two broad factors: (i) the endowments of natural and other resources and (ii) nation-states' long-term strategies/goals/policies. Indeed, that is exactly what has been observed in the real world. First, agricultural trade has occurred in accordance with differences in the endowments of natural resources and production factors (land, soil, climate, water, labor, capital), which determined whether or not a country possesses natural comparative advantage in agriculture[1]. This type of trade has played an immensely important role in

[1] While the endowments of natural resources are likely to remain relatively unchanged over time, the quantity of other production factors such as skilled and unskilled labor and physical, human, and financial capital is expected to change substantially as economies undergo

matching countries with food shortages to countries with food surpluses. For example, countries in the temperate climate zones import tropical fruits and vegetables from countries in the tropical and semi-tropical zones. There is near complete specialization of production for tropical commodities (e.g., coffee, banana, cocoa, mango) across the world. Countries in the arid and semi-arid regions constrained by water shortages have innate disadvantages in producing food grains and therefore they import the bulk of what they eat from foreign countries. In East Asian countries such as Japan and Korea, food/feed crop production costs are significantly higher than other regions given their limited arable lands and therefore import more than 70 percent for Korea and 50 percent for Japan of what they eat from foreign countries.

Second, agricultural trade has occurred owing to artificial advantages or disadvantages constructed during the postwar period by various types of government policies including taxing/subsidizing and public support systems including R&D investments and extension services. There is huge literature on the political economy of agricultural protection and it clearly shows how government policies have shaped domestic agricultural production, distorted international markets, depressed international commodity prices, and became the source of major international disputes through WTO multilateral trade negotiations (Gardner 1992, Binswanger 1997, Anderson, Rausser and Swinnen 2013). The total monetary amount of the distortions of agricultural trade (deadweight losses) has peaked at about $300 billion in 2005 from OECD countries. The literature presents several stylized facts: the size of agricultural protection is in proportion to per capita GDP (industrialized countries subsidize their agricultural sector most heavily); poor countries tax their agricultural sector (negative protection); as their economy develops, they grow to subsidize their agricultural sector (positive protection). In fact, many African countries used to be net food exporting countries before the 1980s despite taxing the agricultural sector. However they turned into net food importing countries after undergoing sets of policies targeted at trade liberalization, privatization, and deregulation associated with the structural adjustment programs imposed by the World Bank and IMF in the 1980s and 1990s.

In contrast, the EU and the US have grown as major food grain exporters in part as a consequence of extensive government support and subsidies (domestic and export) in the postwar period. Such government intervention in

structural transformations from low-income to high-income countries. The change will then bring about a shift in the initial status of comparative advantage.

developed countries has remained virtually unchanged even after the implementation of the Uruguay Agreements on Agriculture (URAA), creating/ sustaining policy-induced artificial comparative advantages.

According to the WTO framework for negotiations, distortions in agricultural trade result from three primary sources: (i) export-promoting subsidies, (ii) import restrictions (market access) including tariffs and nontariff barriers, and (iii) domestic subsidies (market deficiency payment, direct payment) and supply management programs (payment for setting aside arable lands). While it is relatively straightforward to measure trade distortions arising from the first and second sources, there could be controversies about whether and how the third source (domestic policies/programs) is trade-distorting. The WTO devised the so-called 'box system' to address such controversies. The box system divides domestic policies/programs into blue, amber, and green boxes based on whether or not farm policies are decoupled from production decisions or prices. Amber box refers to a group of policies that influences farmers' production decisions or market prices and subject to reductions over a specified period of time with the goal of eventual phase-out. Blue box refers to programs that are used along with production restraints and currently exempt from reduction requirements. If a domestic program belongs to the green box (e.g., crop insurance, environmental protection, extension services, rural development), it is supposed to be decoupled from production decisions; minimally trade-distorting; and not subject to reduction requirements (that is, WTO member countries can use unlimited amounts of fiscal outlays as payments for green box policies).

In efforts to decouple their policies, developed countries have been shifting since 1994 their farm policies from price supports and deficiency payments to direct payments; and from current acres/yields to historical acres/yields in calculating the amounts of payment to farm producers. Nevertheless, research shows that the effects of decoupling has been very modest and green box policies still caused overproduction, continuing to distort trade (Baffes and de Gorter 2005). Jostling (2004) points out three channels through which supposedly decoupled policies may exert influences on production decisions: (i) any payment may encourage production if it relieves income constraints on investment, (ii) even when payments are based on historical acres and yields, expectations of the eventual reassessment of those bases can cause farmers to retain land in production of particular crops, and (iii) safety-net policies that reduce the downside risk of fluctuations in income clearly can have an effect of keeping resources in farming.

Such distorting effects of green box policies are suspected to have reinforced the uneven playing field underlying the current structure of agricultural trade that has been created in the second half of the 20th century by the history of taxing in the developing world (although later they started to protect their agriculture using tariffs but not out of government budgets) and subsidizing in the developed world (Gonzalez 2002, Gonzalez 2004, Stringer 2000, United Nations 2009). The suspicion is closely associated with the different nature of agricultural protection between the two groups of countries. That is, developing countries have relied mostly on border measures (tariffs) for the protection of their agriculture rather than using government budgets because of their lack of budgetary capabilities. Further, the structural adjustment programs and the AoA forced them to reduce their average tariff rates significantly from 30 percent during the 1980s to 15 percent during the 1990s, whereas developed countries did not have to reduce their support significantly given that they were allowed to use unlimited amounts of fiscal outlays (for green box policies) for supporting the agricultural sector. The uneven playing field has resulted in a widened schism between developed and least developed countries in their agricultural production capabilities, making many of them (which used to be self-reliant) dependent on food imports for feeding their people. In sum, the current pattern of agricultural trade embodies both natural comparative advantages and policy-induced artificial comparative advantages, demonstrating that trade pattern is not exclusively shaped by natural resources and factor endowments but may be constructed over time by deliberate government strategies, as alluded by the infant industry protection argument and strategic trade theory.

Short-Run and Long-Run Effects of Agricultural Trade Liberalization

Agricultural trade has been shrinking over the last decades relative to the manufacturing sector. Trade in agriculture represented above 30 percent of all merchandise trade prior to the 1960s before declining to just about 6 percent in 2006 (it rose to 9 percent in 2009 due to the food price crisis of 2007/2008) (Sandri, Valenzuela and Anderson 2007, Anderson 2010). Further, less than 10 percent of what is produced in agricultural sectors across the world is traded internationally compared to 47 percent in the manufacturing sector. Trade barriers in the manufacturing sector have been continuously lowered through successive rounds of GATT trade negotiations starting from Dillon Round to Kennedy Round to Tokyo Round. The average tariff rate in the manufacturing sector declined from 15 percent in the 1980s to about 5 percent in 2010. Although the declining share of agricultural trade is attributable to some extent to increases in the share of consumers' expenditure on nonfood goods as their income rises, agricultural protectionism has also contributed to further constraining the growth of agricultural trade. The consequent mandate of the WTO was to bring together member countries and induce them to commit to a multilateral deal that would significantly reduce barriers to agricultural trade, thereby cutting trade distortions and improving the efficiency of resource allocations at the global scale.

Let's suppose that the WTO were able to abolish all trade-distorting barriers (tariffs, domestic subsidies, and export subsidies) in agriculture across the world. The effects of such a sweeping liberalization could be distinguished between the short- and long-run. In the short-run, the effects of trade liberalization would largely reflect the influence of today's static comparative advantages or disadvantages as shaped by both natural resources and factor endowments and past government policies/strategies. Initially, thanks to the elimination of export and domestic subsidies in developed countries, production of agricultural commodities would decline there, while the elimination of tariffs would increase demand and production elsewhere. Accordingly the prices would rise if the decreased production in developed countries is larger than the increased production elsewhere. It is estimated that the prices would rise initially worsening the food insecurity problem for people living with incomes less than $2 per day in poor countries. Trade would expand substantially and the Cairns group countries (Argentina, Brazil, Thailand, Vietnam, South Africa) and agriculturally abundant developed countries such as New Zealand and Australia are likely to experience substantial expansions in their agricultural sectors, while other developed countries in Europe and East Asia undergoing contractions. Many countries in Sub-Saharan Africa and South Asia are expected to experience contractions in their production given their losing of preferential (most favored nations; MFN) status to markets in developed countries and increase their food imports due to their lack of competitiveness in agriculture at the present time.

Some net food-importing countries in Europe and Asia may face gradual phase-out of domestic agricultural production given their structural disadvantages associated with unfavorable natural resources endowments and consequent high production costs.

The long-term outcomes would depend not only on today's comparative advantages but also on dynamic comparative advantages that would be shaped over time in accordance with the goals and strategies each country may pursue in the long-term regarding the agricultural sector (see Moon, Shin and Pino (2015) in this book for a detailed account of why the state, but not firm level strategies becomes the major determinant of agricultural trade pattern). In other words, while the long-term trade pattern in agriculture would be still subject to natural comparative advantages to a significant extent, states may be able to shift it through strategic investments in agricultural infrastructure and extension services that may help reduce agricultural production costs or improve productivity significantly. Therefore, it is not straightforward to make a prediction of what agricultural trade pattern would look like in the long-term. There may be states that would be willing to allocate more resources to supporting the agricultural sector and foster more domestic production than would be under the prevailing comparative advantage, while other states may not be willing to commit to agriculture, thereby going along with whatever international markets would dictate and willing to accept potential contractions in their agricultural sectors. However, given the strategic and special roles that food plays in international politics, there may be many countries desiring to invest in agriculture and support domestic agriculture (as most countries do today) using policies/programs compatible with the prevailing WTO regime, thereby attempting to attain the highest domestic production feasible within their domestic political, economic, and ecological systems.

Given such uncertainties, we can envisage two diverging results in the long-term from agricultural trade liberalization. The first scenario is that Sub-Saharan African countries would emerge as net exporters given their cheap labors; huge open markets in developed countries; and unexploited potential of agricultural production in the region at the expense of the agriculture of some developed countries in Europe and East Asia, thereby achieving greater specialization of production across the world. This prediction is contingent on proactive and effective roles of the governments of African countries in making sustained investments in the agricultural sector in areas like helping input markets (machines; credit; chemicals) rise and function well; risk sharing; and providing elementary/secondary/tertiary education, extension services, health services and social safety nets; providing physical infrastructures (roads; harbors). Then, Sub-Saharan Africa may emerge as a competitive agricultural producing region in the near future.

That is, with the markets in developed countries wide open, African agriculture can be nourished up for the task of meeting the global challenge of increasing food production by utilizing high yielding varieties seed, fertilizers, irrigation technology and infrastructure that are commonly used in other parts of the world (Thurow 2010). Then, countries in Africa along with those in Latin America and Southeast Asia may end up taking a larger share of agricultural exports. Australia, New Zealand, Canada, the US are likely to strengthen their position as agricultural exporters whereas some countries in Europe and East Asia may have to depend on international markets for most of its food supply. The second scenario is that food insecure countries in Africa and South Asia remain dependent on food imports even after the full liberalization of agricultural trade, indicating that their agricultural sectors would have failed to grow to gain international competitiveness. This scenario may arise due to three possibilities: (i) the current uneven playing field in international trade rules is too much for African countries to overcome and grow to successfully compete with the agriculture of food-exporting developed or middle-income countries; (ii) inabilities or ineffectiveness of the governments of African countries in providing infrastructure needed for enhancing agricultural productivity and institutions needed for constructing markets for credits, risks, and other inputs; (iii) developed countries have greater capacity to invest in agriculture than developing or least developed countries and they have strong commitment to helping their agriculture in terms of R and D investment and extension services, hence they maintain sustainable competitive advantage in agriculture. In addition, developed countries are expected to better cope with potentially harmful effects of climate change than developing or least developed countries. This second scenario of Sub-Saharan Africa remaining dependent on food imports would not be a big problem from the perspective of the global food insecurity problem if Africa were able to achieve sustained economic growth as a consequence of reallocating more of their resources to manufacturing and industrial sectors which have comparative advantage and substantially improve their income, say, to the level of middle-income countries. However, this scenario is not highly likely given the strong empirical evidence demonstrating that agricultural growth is an antecedent for industrialization and overall economic growth (to be shown in the next section).

Global Food Security and Agricultural Trade

The above analysis indicates that the effectiveness of government actions in food insecure countries would play a decisive role in determining whether in the long-run agricultural trade liberalization would be helpful for them in increasing agricultural production. If states take necessary steps for agricultural growth and development, their agricultural sector has the potential to rise as a competitive agricultural production region and become net agricultural exporters, thereby reducing/eliminating food insecurity in the regions. Due to the following two reasons, agricultural growth and development in the region is indispensable for promoting global food security.

First, research shows that agricultural growth plays an indispensable role for industrialization and overall economic growth. Historically speaking, all developed and middle-income countries have commonly undergone robust growths in agricultural productivity prior to or at least simultaneously with industrialization processes. African countries have unsuccessfully attempted during the 1980s and 1990s to bypass agriculture and achieve industrialization directly, causing their economies to lag far behind other developing countries. They dismantled state marketing board and government subsidies to the agricultural sector (credit, fertilizer, machines), and substantially reduced public investment needed for building agricultural infrastructure and support systems. The detrimental effects on African agriculture of liberalization, privatization, and lack of public efforts to build food system infrastructure have impeded industrialization and retarded the overall economy. The literature presents robust evidence underlining the need for growing the agricultural sector as a development strategy (Bhagwati and Srinivasan 1975, Eicher and Staatz 1984, Dowrick and Gemmell 1991, Datt and Ravallion 1998, Thirtle, Lin and Piesse 2003, Gollin, Pabente and Rogerson 2002, Tiffin and Irz 2006, Gollin, Parente and Rogerson 2007 and Awokuse 2009). In particular, Gollin, Pabente, and Rogerson (2002) show that agricultural productivity growth explains a substantial portion of the growth of per capita GDP for developing countries and demonstrates that per capita GDP growth can be decomposed into agriculture (54 percent), followed by sectoral shifts (29 percent) and manufacturing sector (17 percent). For developed countries, they show that improvements in the productivity of nonagricultural sectors would determine economic growth in the long-run. The studies above illustrate that the absence/lack of growth in agricultural production and productivity would result in poor performances in overall economic growth and it is not likely to be feasible to have economic growth/development without first achieving agricultural growth.

Second, known as the pro-poor growth, agricultural growth is particularly effective in reducing the poverty/hunger rates in developing countries. With the benefits of economic growth often not transmitted to people living with less than $1 a day and more than two-thirds of the poor people live in farm/rural areas, agriculture is an industry that can make the strongest effect on ameliorating poverty by increasing farm/rural incomes via increased agricultural production/productivity. In consideration of these multiple roles of agriculture in a development process, Timmer (2005) noted that an agriculture-driven growth strategy, if it does not sacrifice aggregate growth, directs a greater share of income to the poor; i.e., it is more pro-poor," thereby placing agriculture at the center of the pro-poor development strategy. In support of Timmer, strong empirical literature highlight a positive linkage between improvements in agricultural productivity and poverty reduction (e.g., Irz, Lin, Thirtle and Wiggins 2001, Thirtle, Lin and Piesse 2002, Ravallion and Datt 1996, Fan, Hazell and Thorat 2000, Christiaensen et al. 2006). Given such strong quantitative/statistical evidence confirming the role of agriculture in poverty reduction, policy-makers in developing countries, donor countries, and international development organizations have started to pay renewed interest to agriculture (Timmer 2005).

The upshot is that agricultural trade liberalization would be immensely beneficial for redressing the global food insecurity problem in the developing world by boosting agricultural growth, reducing poverty and hunger, and laying the foundation for industrialization and overall economic development (assuming that states make persistent investments in infrastructure necessary for efficient functioning of agricultural markets). However, considering the outcomes of the GATT/WTO multilateral trade negotiations over the last decades, such a scenario of full liberalization of agricultural trade across the world is next to impossible. As noted earlier, the diversity of agricultural roles across different regions/countries coupled with the entrenched domestic politics surrounding farm protection makes it extremely difficult for all countries to accept one-size-fit-all rules for trade.

The GATT/WTO approach in response to such difficulty of liberalizing agricultural trade has been to introduce exceptions (to the principle of free trade) so that various countries/regions can pursue strategies that suit their unique individual needs. For example, the traffic light box system is designed to help the developed world to address issues related to the notion of multifunctional agriculture while attempting to reduce trade distortion.

For developing and least developed countries are the special and differential treatment (SDT) provisions. The SDT provisions call for developed countries to provide preferential access to developing countries, permitting them to be to a varying degree exempted from reduction commitments in the three areas of domestic support, export subsidies, and market access. The SDT, however, suffers from problems including; (i) it is too general to be of realistic assistance to developing countries; (ii) it is only a transitory institution compared to the box system of much more perpetuity, (iii) it is concessionary, and (iii) it fails to create incentives for long-term investments critical for agricultural developments in LDCs; and (iv) it may justify the continuation of agricultural protectionism in developed countries and abate the motivation for global trade reforms (Hoekman, Michalopoulos and Winters 2004, Badiane 2007, Weis 2007). Outside of the WTO, the EU devised various preferential status rules designated for former colonies in Africa and exempting tariffs and other restrictions on imports from them.

The newest additions to the list of exceptions include ‘special products’ and special safeguard against import surges for developing countries and ‘sensitive products’ for developed countries. Hence, the current WTO attempts to recognize the special roles of agriculture different than the manufacturing sector and different roles of agriculture across countries at varying developmental stages. Given the diverse roles of agriculture over the course of economic development over time and across countries with sharp divergences in income, the number of exceptions has kept growing during the WTO trade negotiations, initially meant to make it easier to reach a multilateral deal but now making it much more complicated to negotiate and reach a deal.

In sum, the current WTO trade rules represent a set of compromises among the ideal of free trade, special aspects of agriculture, and conflicts of national/agricultural interests across countries. Yet they are more aligned with the agricultural interests of the developed world, making the agriculture of the least developed countries vulnerable as manifested by the transitory nature of the SDT provisions in contrast to the box system as a permanent institution permitting developed countries to use decoupled subsidies unlimited. Hence, the current trade rules under the WTO are detrimental to promoting global food security.

If the highest priority of our world is to ensure food security in every corner of the world at any costs, the best strategy for the promotion of global food security would be for developed countries to unilaterally liberalize their agriculture, while permitting food insecure developing countries to protect and nurture their agriculture using policy instruments needed including tariffs and domestic subsidies as developed countries have done since WWII. While expected to shrink the agriculture of many developed countries and harm their farm interests substantially (hence realistically not very feasible), that would be much more effective in promoting global food security than the one-size-fits-all trade liberalization. When following the full liberalization scenario, developing or least developed countries would not be allowed to use policy instruments that are imperative for nurturing their agricultural sector when such instruments violate the rules of free trade, therefore slowing down the process of agricultural growth. There are diverse efforts from the developed world to assist the least developed countries (LDCs) to achieve faster economic growth such as the official development assistance (ODA), food aid, foreign direct investments, private foundations funds, and the United Nations World Food Programme. The fact is that reforming the current WTO trade rules toward allowing food insecure developing countries to protect/support their agriculture will do much more than all such efforts combined in ameliorating global food insecurity.

Some proponents of free trade in agriculture argue that food insecure developing countries can rely on international markets and cheap food imports to ensure food security (Runge and Senauer 2000, Tweeten 1999). This argument has flaws from the following perspectives. Food-importing developing countries may experience financial hardships in procuring food in international markets if they were not successful in raising their incomes through the growth of other industrial sectors (that is, if they were not able to take advantage of the potentially greater efficiency of resource reallocation to nonagricultural sectors). As emphasized earlier, food importing developing countries are not likely to achieve economic growth/development without first undergoing agricultural growth. Therefore, continued food dependence on foreign imports (or lack of significant improvements in agricultural productivity) would mean that they would not have been successful in generating sustained economic growth. Further, considering that global food commodity markets are often dominated by a few large multinational trading corporations and international prices may significantly diverge from competitive prices, food insecure developing countries may be placed in financially even more vulnerable positions. The financial ability to access international food markets could become a bigger problem under a very specialized international agricultural production system if natural disasters (more likely in this climate change era) hit a region of major agricultural exporting countries and cause sharp increases in international food commodity prices.

The above concerns are not distant possibilities but we experienced them just a few years ago during the 2007/2008 and 2011 food price crises and likely in the future, too.

CONCLUSION

The foundation for international trade in agriculture was laid by the repeal of the Corn Laws in 1846 and the Navigation Acts in 1849 and subsequent spread of economic liberalism of the 19th century. European states tended to move toward freer trade in agriculture between the 1840s and 1870s. The flow of agricultural trade has been from colonial countries in Africa to Europe for tropical commodities and from new settler countries (the US, Australia, Canada) for food grains and meat products to Europe. Except for such imports and exports, agricultural production in most countries in the 19th century were for domestic consumption rather than exporting. During the postwar period, the policy direction of the developing world has favored urban consumers and the manufacturing sector while taxing their agricultural sector given the lack of political power of the agricultural sector relative to the urban and manufacturing interests. Despite such a burden, the agricultural sector in Africa remained exporters until the 1970s. In contrast, developed countries intervened in agricultural markets in order to boost farm incomes and vitalize rural economies (farm support in the US starting during the Great Depression era and in Europe in the 1960s in the form of the Common Agricultural Policy (CAP) as part of the broad goal of consolidating unity and peace in the region. A wide range of policy instruments has been used including supply management (land set aside programs), variable levy system, price supports, deficiency payment, direct payment, crop insurance, risk management tools, import tariffs, tariff rate quotas, export subsidies, and environmental conservation programs.

The protection (combination of subsidies from fiscal outlays, tariffs, and export subsidies) of the agricultural sector in developed countries caused massive overproduction and depressed commodity prices in international markets, contributing to converting many food exporting developing countries to food importers and some countries in Europe as major food exporting countries. Following the trade rules (traffic light box system) of the AoA from the Uruguay Round, developed countries reduced the use of market- and trade-distorting policy instruments while increasing the use of decoupled and minimally distorting instruments, risk management and safety nets programs. However, barely rectifying the overproduction problems, the change did not signal a fundamental shift in their policy to fully embracing market-oriented reforms. The developing world, however, had to undergo substantial reductions in tariffs and other non-tariff barriers through the process of tariffication, opening their domestic markets to exports from developed countries.

Such postwar history of agricultural policies around the world in combination with the institution of WTO trade rules and the structural adjustment programs associated with the Washington Consensus in the 1980s and 1990s have resulted in the current uneven playing field and trade pattern in agricultural commodities, which involves the following disparate groups of countries: (i) the artificially strong agricultural sector in the EU nurtured and maintained by state intervention, (ii) naturally strong (and state supported) agricultural sectors in high-income (e.g., US, Canada, New Zealand, Australia) and middle-income countries (e.g., Brazil, Argentina, Indonesia, Malaysia, Viet Nam, Thailand), (iii) naturally uncompetitive agricultural sectors in food-importing high-income countries (e.g., Japan, Korea, Norway, Swiss, Taiwan), (iv) food-importing developing and least developed countries in Africa and South Asia. The number of food insecure people is the largest in Sub-Saharan Africa and South Asia, posing the greatest challenge in promoting global food security.

Proponents for free trade argue that trade liberalization in agriculture would be conducive in the long term to helping the agricultural sector in food insecure developing countries grow, reduce poverty, and contribute to redressing the global food insecurity problem. We concur with the argument, but with the caveat that the state should play an effective role in guiding the process of agricultural development (hence, free trade in agriculture should not be equated with *laissez-faire*). They further argue that unilateral trade liberalization by the developing world would generate significant gains for itself. This argument has a major flaw. In the case of the unilateral liberalization, developing countries would receive the gains predominantly in the form of enhanced consumers' welfare that stems from a reallocation of resources more aligned with the static comparative advantage but at the expense of the agricultural production sector by exposing it to greater competition when it really needs protection and nourishment from the government. That is, there may be short-term benefits to food consumers but in the long-term food insecure developing countries may be deprived of the opportunity to grow its agricultural production capacity and lay the groundwork for industrialization.

Agricultural growth represents a strategy that is most effective for reducing poverty/hunger and permitting people living under one dollar a day to access sufficient amounts of food. It should be emphasized, however, that agricultural growth requires a proactive support by the state in various ways including the provision of physical infrastructure, irrigation, extension services, and the facilitation of the rise of the markets for credits, risks, and other essential inputs for agricultural production.

The mission of the WTO was to undo the interventions and distortions states have done in the postwar period (dismantle agricultural protection around the world to achieve a global system of specialized production), thereby creating a trade pattern that would be determined by comparative advantages.

The experiences of the last few decades, however, show that the mission is next to impossible with the Doha Round multilateral trade negotiations in deadlock without much hope of making significant progress in reducing trade barriers in agriculture. We contend then that the next best strategy of promoting global food security is to repair the uneven playing field and permit the governments of food insecure developing countries to subsidize and support their agricultural sector.

As mentioned earlier, the special and differential treatments (SDT) provisions are temporary and not legally binding, hence a weak instrument as a mechanism designed to provide food insecure developing countries with the opportunity to advance their agricultural development. We contend that the WTO should institute a permanent mechanism for food insecure developing countries much like the traffic light box system which permits the developed world to support and subsidize the agricultural sector unlimited for the purpose of promoting the provision of multifunctional goods and services.

An example of such a mechanism for food insecure developing countries could be the Development/Food Security Box, which has been proposed by groups of developing countries during the Doha Round negotiations but discarded given the objections from other groups of countries. The Development/Food Security Box would help small scale farmers in need of resources and stable supplies of staple foods by allowing food insecure developing countries to use higher tariffs and safeguards to promote greater domestic production of staple crops while outlawing developed countries' dumping of agricultural products (WTO 2002, Braun et al. 2002, Ruffer et al. 2002). We believe that mechanisms like the Development/Food Security Box could fix the uneven playing field in agricultural trade and offer a promising avenue to promote global food security in the absence of the full liberalization of agricultural trade.

References

Anderson, K., W. Martin and D. van der Mensbrugghe. Distortions to World Trade: Impacts on Agricultural Markets and Farm Incomes. *Review of Agricultural Economics* 28 (2006).

Awokuse, T. O. Does Agriculture Really Matter for Economic Growth in Developing Countries? *Selected paper presented at the Applied Agricultural Economics Association Annual Meeting*, Milwaukee, WI, July 28 2009.

Chang, H. J. 2009. Rethinking public policy in agriculture: lessons from history, distant and recent. *Journal of Peasant Studies* 36, 477-515.

Collier, P. 2008. Facing the global problems of development. In: Alexandroff, A. S. (Ed.), *Can the World Be Governed: Possibilities for Effective Multilateralism*. Wilfrid Laurier University Press.

Echevarria, C. Changes in Sectoral Composition Associated with Economic Growth. *International Economic Review* 38 (1997) 431-452.

Fan, S., Hazell, P. and Thorat, S. Government Spending, Growth, and Poverty in India. *Ameircan Journal of Agricultural Economics* 82 (2000): 1038-1051.

FAO. The State of Food and Agriculture in Asia and the Pacific Region, RAP Publication, Bangkok, Thailand. 2008.

Fei, C. H. and G. Ranis. Innovation, Capital Accumulation and Economic Development. *American Economic Review* 53 (1963): 283-313.

Felipe, J. Total Factor Productivity Growth in East Asia: A Critical Survey. *EDRC Report Series No. 65*, Asian Development Bank 1997. 26.

Fulginiti, L. E. and R. K. Perrin. Agricultural Productivity in Developing Countries. *Agricultural Economics* 19 (1998): 45-51.

Fabiosa, J., Beghin, J., de Cara, S., Elobeid, A., Fang, C., Isik, M., Mattey, H., Saak, A., Westhoff, P., Brown, D. S., Willott, B., Madison, D., Meyer, S., Kruse, J. 2005. The Doha round of the world trade organization and agricultural markets liberalization: impacts on developing economies. *Review of Agricultural Economics* 27, 317-335.

Gemmell, T., A. Lloyd and M. Mathew. Agricultural Growth and Inter-Sectoral Linkages in a Developing Economy. *Journal of Agricultural Economics* 51 (2000): 352-370.

Godfray, H. C., Beddington, J. R., Crute, I. R., Haddad, L., Lawrence, D., Muir, J. F., Pretty, J., Robinson, S., Thomas, S. M., Toulmin, C. 2010. Food security: the challenge of feeding 9 billion people. *Science* 327, 812-818.

Gollin, D., S. L. Parente and R. Rogerson. The Role of Agriculture in Development. *American Economic Review, Proceedings* 92 (2002): 160-164.

Gollin, D., S. L. Parente and R. Rogerson. The Food Problem and the Evolution of International Income Levels. *Journal of Monetary Economics* 54 (2007): 1230-1255.

Gonzalez, C. G. 2002. Institutionalizing inequality: the WTO agreement on agriculture, food security, and developing countries. *Columbia Journal of Environmental Law* 27, 433 (Available at SSRN) http://ssrn.com/abstract=987945.

Gonzalez, C. G. 2004. Trade liberalization, food security and the environment: the neoliberal threat to sustainable rural development. *Transnational Law and Contemporary Problems 14* (Available at SSRN) http://ssrn.com/abstract=987150.

Gonzalez, C. G. 2006. Deconstructing the mythology of free trade: critical reflections on comparative advantage. *Berkeley La Raza Law Journal 65.*

Grossman, G. M., Krueger, A. 1995. Economic growth and the environment. *Quarterly Journal of Economics* 110, 353 377.

Gullison, R. E., Frumhoff, P. C., Canadell, J. G., Field, C. B., Nepstad, D. C., Hayhoe, K., Avissar, R., Curran, L. M., Friedlingstein, P., Jones, C. D., Nobre, C. 2007. Tropical forests and climate policy. *Science* 316, 985-986.

Hoekman, B., Michalopoulos, C., Winters, L. A. 2004. Special and differential treatment of developing countries in the WTO: moving foreword after Cancun. *World Economy* 27, 481-506.

IAASTD. *International Assessment of Agricultural Knowledge, Science and Technology for Development: Global Report. 2009.* Ed. by B. McIntyre, H. Herren, J. Wakhungu, R. T. Watson.

Ingco, M. D. 1995. Agricultural trade liberalization in the Uruguay round: one step foreword, one step back? *Policy Research Working Paper*. The World Bank.

Johnson, D. G. 1987. World agriculture in disarray revisited. *Australian Journal of Agricultural Economics* 31 142-153.

Josling, T. 2004. Domestic farm policies and the WTO negotiations on domestic support. In: Anania, G., Bohman, M. E., Carter, C. A., McCalla, A. F. (Eds.), *From Agricultural Policy Reform and the WTO: Where Are We Heading?* Edward Elgar.

Kim, D. H. and S. C. Lin. Trade and Growth at Different Stages of Economic Development. *Journal of Development Studies* 45 (2008): 1211-1224.

Koning, N. 2007. What can be learned from the history of developed countries? In: Koning, N., Pinstrup-Andersen, P. (Eds.), *Agricultural Trade Liberalization and the Least Developed Countries*. Springer.

Koning, N., Pinstrup-Adndersen, P. 2007. Agricultural trade liberalization and the least developed countries. In: Koning, N., Pinstrup-Andersen, P. (Eds.), *Agricultural Trade Liberalization and the Least Developed Countries*. Springer.

Krugman, P. R. 1986. *Strategic Trade Policy and the New International Economics*. The MIT Press, Cambridge, Mass.

Krugman, P. R. 1987. Is free trade passe? *Economic Perspectives* 1 131-144.

Kym, A., Martin, W. 2005. Agricultural trade reform and the doha development agenda. *The World Economy* 28 1301-1327.

McCalla, A. F. 1969. Protectionism in international agricultural trade. *Agricultural History* 43, 327-344.

McCalla, A. F. 1993. Agricultural trade liberalization: the ever-elusive grail. *American Journal of Agricultural Economics* 75 1102-1112.

McCalla, A. F. 1999. Prospects for food security in the 21st century: with emphasis on Africa. *Agricultural Economics* 20, 95-103.

McCalla, A. F. 2003. Liberalizing agricultural trade: will it ever be a reality? *Journal of Agricultural and Resource Economics* 28, 410-434.

Michalopoulos, C. 2004. Rules and options for special and differential treatment. In: Ingco, M. D., Nash, J. D. (Eds.), *Agriculture and the WTO: Creating a Trading System for Development*. World Bank and Oxford University Press.

Millenium Ecosystem Assessment 2005. The United Nations.

North, D. C. Economic Performance Through Time. *American Economic Review* 84 (1994): 359-368.

Panagariya, A. 2002. Developing countries at Doha: a political economy analysis. *World Economy* 1205-1233.

Pingali, P. Agriculture Renaissance: Making "Agriculture for Development" Work in the 21st Century. *Handbook of Agricultural Economics*, Volume 4. 2010.

Rosegrant, M., Cline, S. A. 2003. Global food security: challenges and policies. *Science* 302 1917-1918.

Self, S. and R. Grabowski. Economic Development and the Role of Agricultural Technology. *Agricultural Economics* 36 (2007): 395-404.

Stiglitz, J., E. Markets, Market Failures and Development. *American Economic Review* 79 (1989): 197-210.

Stiglitz, J. E. Globalization, Technology, and Asian Development. *Asian Development Review* 20 (2003): 1-18.

Swinnen, J. F. M., A Positive Theory of Agricultural Protection. *American Journal of Agricultural Economics* 76 (1994): 1-14.

Swinnen, J. F. M., Van Der Zee, F. A. 1993. The political economy of agricultural policies. *European Review of Agricultural Economics* 20 261-290.

Thirtle, C., L. Lin and J. Piesse. The Impact of Research-Led Agricultural Productivity Growth on Poverty Reduction in Africa, Asia and Latin America. *World Development* 31 (2006):1959-1975.

Thurow, R. 2010. The fertile continent: Africa, agriculture's final frontier. *Foreign Affairs* (November/December).

Tiffin, R., X. Irz. Is Agriculture the Engine of Growth? *Agricultural Economics* 35: 79-89.

Timmer, C. P. Getting Agriculture Moving: Do Markets Provide the Right Signals. *Food Policy* 20 (1995): 455-472.

Timmer, C. P. 2005. Agriculture and pro-poor growth. *Center for Global Development. Working paper # 63.*

Timmer, C. P. 2010. The agricultural transformation. In: Chenery, H., Srinivasan, T. N. (Eds.), *From Handbook of Development Economics*, vol. 1. Elsevier Science.

Weis, T. 2007. *The Global food economy: the battle for the future of farming.* Zed Books. Fernwood Publishing, London.

In: Trade Liberalization
Editor: Pauline Santos

ISBN: 978-1-63483-867-2

Chapter 2

Corporate Social Responsibility, Trade Liberalization and Global Welfare

Angela C. Chao[1,*], Jen-yao Lee[2] and Leonard F. S. Wang[3,4]

[1]Department of Economics, Southeast University, Nanjing, China
[2]Department of International Business, National Kaohsiung University of Applied Science, Kaohsiung, Taiwan
[3]Wenlan School of Business, Zhongnan University of Economics and Law, Wuhan, China
[4]SinoAsia Economic and Management Foundation, Taiwan

Abstract

In an international duopolistic market, the consumer-oriented CSR initiatives will make the domestic government lower the tariff rate if the weight is relatively high in both cases of dual CSR and unilateral CSR by the foreign firm; however, the government will raise the tariff rate if the weight is relatively high in the case of unilateral CSR by the domestic firm. Furthermore, the consumer-oriented CSR initiative of both firms is the dominant strategy if the CSR cost is sufficiently low. More importantly, the consumer-oriented CSR initiative of both firms is the

---

* E-mail: angela_zc@seu.edu.cn.

global social welfare optimum if the CSR cost is sufficiently low coupled with trade liberalization.

Keywords: tariff protection, corporate social responsibility, rent-shifting effect, global welfare, trade liberalization
JEL codes: F12, M14, L21

1. INTRODUCTION

In the December 2006 issue of *Harvard Business Review*, Porter and Kramer present a systematic analysis linking competitive advantage to corporate social responsibility (CSR), and explain how a company can use competitive strategy to plumb the opportunity of corporate social responsibility--and in the process enhance its own long-term competitiveness while producing much more social-needed good than traditional CSR does. The authors also point out two key reasons why many companies which have launched CSR efforts find these efforts not as much productive as they could be. One reason is that these companies simply consider CSR as "a cost, a constraint, or a charitable deed" (p. 2). The other reason is that these companies do not incorporate CSR efforts as parts of their core business strategies. It is often that due to the consumer sovereignty in market operation, the competing firms are "altruistic" or "consumer-friendly" in that consumer preferences enter directly into the objective functions of their business operations. In view of these observations, we present an economic approach to analyze the potential efficacy of CSR as a management strategy when markets are characterized by imperfect competition in international trade framework.

Corporate social responsibility (CSR), originating from the expectations of the society for business adopting appropriate business behavior and outcomes (Wood 1991), has received increasing attention from firms and researchers in the past several decades. The literature has provided numerous interesting perspectives on the aspects of CSR. One strand of the literature considers CSR as the private provision of public goods and the private elimination of public bads. In general, the obtained results are parallel with those in the literature on the private provision of public goods, (e.g., Bagnoli and Watts 2003; Kotchen 2006; Besley and Ghatak 2007). Another strand of the literature investigates the possible motivations of firms in adopting CSR (e.g., Baron 2001; Baron 2009; Porter and Kramer 2006; Benabou and Tirole 2010). In particular, Baron argues that firms can adopt pure CSR for altruistic reasons or they adopt strategic CSR for reasons related to self-interest, public politics, and private politics. When firms anticipate that using strategic CSR as a “doing-well-by-doing-good” strategy can improve their competitive position in the market, they should seize any opportunity to adopt CSR.[†]

The above studies have indicated that CSR is increasingly becoming a significant part of modern companies, but relatively little research has been done to analyze its economic effects within the framework of international competition. This notion of the consumer-oriented CSR commitment is in parallel with that of consumer-friendly initiative. Wang et al. (2012) analyze how tariffs and welfare of an importing third country are affected by consumer-friendly foreign exporters. Among the interesting findings of their study are as follows: foreign exporters that care about their profits and consumer surplus are willing to increase their exports and lower their prices, as compare to the case when they are purely profit-maximizing firms. In response to the consumer-friendly initiatives of the foreign firms, the importing country’s government lowers tariffs, causing a gain in profits for the firms. In equilibrium, the exporting firms’ consumer-friendly initiative is able to generate a positive outcome since not only firm profits are greater, both consumer surplus and social welfare of the importing country are also increased. The authors stress that in equilibrium there is a win-win-win solution in international trade framework.

Chang et al. (2014) examine the welfare implications of corporate social responsibility (CSR) in international markets under imperfect competition. Based on a stylized model of an import-competing duopolistic market, they show the feasibility of moving toward tariff reduction when both domestic and foreign firms launch the CSR initiatives in that their payoffs include not only individual profits, but also the benefits of consumers. They find that if the foreign exporter unilaterally adopts the consumer-oriented CSR as a strategy, there is a rent-shifting effect because the foreign firm’s payoff increases whereas the domestic firm’s profit decreases. In response, the importing country government raises its tariff on the foreign product. If, instead, the domestic firm adopts the CSR strategy unilaterally, the rent-shifting effect disappears and both the competing firms’ payoffs increase. They identify the conditions under which the consumer-oriented CSR initiatives of the firms constitute the dominant strategy, leading to a win-win-win equilibrium at

[†] See Manasakis et al. (2013) and Liu et al. (2015) respectively examine the certification issue of CSR and ECSR (Environmental Corporate Social Responsibility).

which the firms' payoffs, consumer surplus, and social welfare are at their maximum levels.

In this chapter, we intend to show that the success of competing firms in international markets and the maximization of consumer and social welfare are not a zero-sum game under imperfect competition. We analyze the behavior of firms pursuing not only their own profits, but also the benefits of their consumers. That is, we wish to know how the not-for-profit firms make their output decisions when they have the truly altruistic motivation of pro-consumer behavior. In particular, we consider the import-competing market as in Chang et al. (2014) and explore the import tariff policy when competing firms are engaging in consumer-oriented CSR. There are few scenarios are considered: 1. When both foreign and domestic firms care the consumer-oriented CSR initiatives; 2. When foreign firm cares the consumer-oriented CSR initiatives only; 3. When only domestic firm cares the consumer-oriented CSR. The remainder of the chapter is organized as follows. Section 2 describes the basic model setting. Section 3 provides tariff and welfare analysis under different scenarios. Policy conclusions are provided in Section 4.

2. The Model

Consider a domestic market for a homogeneous good produced by one domestic firm and one foreign firm. The linear demand function is specified as $\mathrm{P} = \mathrm{a} - \mathrm{Q}$. The supply equation is given by $Q = q_i + q_j$, where q_i and q_j denote, respectively, the output of domestic firm and foreign firm. All firms use an identical technology and have increasing marginal cost function: $\frac{q_i^2}{2}$ and $\frac{q_j^2}{2}$, respectively.

The profits of domestic firms and foreign firms without CSR are given by:

$$\pi_i = (a - q_i - q_j)q_i - \frac{q_i^2}{2} \tag{1}$$

$$\pi_j = (a - q_i - q_j - t)q_j - \frac{q_j^2}{2} \tag{2}$$

where t is the tariff rate. Depending on whether the firms incorporate CSR into their output decisions, we have following payoffs (profit or utility):

$$O_i = (a - q_i - q_j)q_i - \frac{q_i^2}{2} + \alpha_i CS - K \tag{3}$$

$$O_j = (a - q_i - q_j - t)q_j - \frac{q_j^2}{2} + \alpha_j CS - K \tag{4}$$

Let α_i and α_j denote the weight of consumer-friendly initiative assigned to the profits in the decision-making process of firm i and firm j. $CS = \frac{Q^2}{2}$ denotes the consumer surplus. The managers take consumer surplus into account if the owner spend K amount in CSR.

The global social welfare and domestic social welfare are

$$GW = SW + O_j \tag{5}$$

$$SW = CS + O_i + tq_j \tag{6}$$

We construct a two-stage game. In the first stage of the game, the domestic government decides the optimal tariff. In the second stage, the firms engage in Cournot competition. The backward induction is used to derive the *sub-game perfect Nash equilibrium* (SPNE).

3. Tariff Policy and Welfare Analysis

The outputs for the domestic firm and the foreign firm are obtained by partially differentiating Eqs. (3) and (4) with respect to q_i and q_j, the first-order conditions are:

$$\frac{\partial O_i}{\partial q_i} = a + q_i(\alpha_i - 3) + q_j(\alpha_i - 1) = 0 \tag{7}$$

$$\frac{\partial O_j}{\partial q_j} = a - t + q_j(\alpha_j - 3) + q_i(\alpha_j - 1) = 0 \tag{8}$$

The equilibrium outputs are:

$$q_i^*(t) = \frac{2a + t + (a - t)\alpha_i - a\alpha_j}{2(4 - \alpha_i - \alpha_j)} \tag{9}$$

$$q_j^*(t) = \frac{2a-3t-(a-t)\alpha_i+a\alpha_j}{2(4-\alpha_i-\alpha_j)} \tag{10}$$

Substituting Eqs. (9) and (10) into Eq. (6) and then differentiating with respect to t, we obtain:

$$\frac{\partial W}{\partial t} = \frac{14a-41t+5(a-t)\alpha_i^2+\alpha_j(a+12t-2a\alpha_j)+\alpha_i(-15a+26t+(a-4t)\alpha_j)}{4(4-\alpha_i-\alpha_j)^2} = 0 \tag{11}$$

$$\frac{\partial^2 W}{\partial t^2} = \frac{\alpha_i(26-5\alpha_i-4\alpha_j)+12\alpha_j-41}{4(4-\alpha_i-\alpha_j)^2} < 0.$$

The optimum tariff rate is that

$$t^* = \frac{a(14+5\alpha_i^2-\alpha_i(15-\alpha_j)+\alpha_j-2\alpha_j^2)}{41-26\alpha_i+5\alpha_i^2-4(3-\alpha_i)\alpha_j} \tag{12}$$

Next, we consider four cases of the firms with and without CSR.

(1) NN, $\alpha_i = \alpha_j = 0$, then

$$t^{NN} = \frac{14a}{41};\ O_i^{NN} = \frac{216a^2}{1681};\ O_j^{NN} = \frac{75a^2}{3362}$$

$$CS^{NN} = \frac{289a^2}{3362};\ SW^{NN} = \frac{21a^2}{82};\ GW^{NN} = \frac{21a^2}{82} + \frac{75a^2}{3362}$$

(2) YY, $\alpha_i = \alpha_j = \alpha$, then

$$t^{YY} = \frac{2a(7+\alpha(2\alpha-7))}{41+\alpha(9\alpha-38)};\ O_i^{YY} = \frac{a^2(4-\alpha)(3-\alpha)(36+\alpha(17\alpha-55))}{2(41+\alpha(9\alpha-38))^2} - K$$

$$O_j^{YY} = \frac{a^2(5-\alpha^2)(15+\alpha(11\alpha-34))}{2(41+\alpha(9\alpha-38))^2} - K;\ CS^{YY} = \frac{a^2(17-7\alpha)^2}{2(41+\alpha(9\alpha-38))^2}$$

$$SW^{YY} = \frac{a^2(21+(\alpha-12)\alpha)}{82+2\alpha(9\alpha-38)} - K$$

$$GW^{YY} = \frac{a^2(21+(\alpha-12)\alpha)}{82+2\alpha(9\alpha-38)} + \frac{a^2(5-\alpha^2)(15+\alpha(11\alpha-34))}{2(41+\alpha(9\alpha-38))^2} - 2K$$

Taking differentiation of t^{YY} with respect to α, we obtain:

$$\frac{\partial t^{YY}}{\partial \alpha} = -\frac{2a(21+\alpha(13\alpha-38))}{(41+\alpha(9\alpha-38))^2} < 0, \text{ if } \alpha > \frac{1}{13}(19-2\sqrt{22}).$$

For symmetric CSR, we have following lemma.

Lemma 1. *The adoption of the CSR strategy by both firms makes them more aggressive on output decision. The government should lower the tariff rate imposing on the foreign product if the weight of consumer-friendly initiative is relatively high.*

The economic intuition is provided via the following two effects: a consumer-oriented CSR creates the well-known "rent-shifting effect" and a new "consumer surplus effect." A foreign firm's consumer-oriented CSR initiative makes it more aggressive in increasing the quantity of its export and creates a "rent-shifting effect" because foreign profit increases whereas domestic profit decreases. In addition, the "consumer surplus effect" due to trade creation will improve domestic social welfare. If the weight is low initially, the "rent-shifting effect" dominates the "consumer surplus effect". Under such circumstances, the domestic government will raise the tariff rate. However, if the weight is high initially and the "consumer surplus effect" dominates the "rent-shifting effect," the domestic government shall lower the tariff rate.

(3) NY, $\alpha_i = 0$ and $\alpha_j = \alpha$, then

$$t^{NY} = \frac{a(\alpha(2\alpha-1)-14)}{12\alpha-41}; \; O_i^{NY} = \frac{3a^2(12-5\alpha)^2}{2(41-12\alpha)^2}$$

$$O_j^{NY} = \frac{a^2(5+3\alpha)(15+\alpha(4\alpha-25))}{2(41-12\alpha)^2} - K$$

$$CS^{NY} = \frac{a^2(17-2\alpha)^2}{2(41-12\alpha)^2}; \; SW^{NY} = \frac{a^2(21+(\alpha-2)\alpha)}{82-24\alpha}$$

$$GW^{NY} = \frac{a^2(21+(\alpha-2)\alpha)}{82-24\alpha} + \frac{a^2(5+3\alpha)(15+\alpha(4\alpha-25))}{2(41-12\alpha)^2} - K$$

Taking differentiation of t^{NY} with respect to α, we obtain:

$$\frac{\partial t^{NY}}{\partial \alpha} = \frac{1}{6}\alpha\left(1 - \frac{127}{(41-12\alpha)^2}\right) < 0, \text{ if } \alpha > \frac{1}{12}(41 - \sqrt{427}).$$

***Lemma* 2.** *The unilateral adoption of the CSR strategy by the foreign firm makes it more aggressive on export decision. The domestic government may lower the tariff rate imposing on the foreign product if the weight of consumer-friendly initiative is relatively high.*

Highly weighting of CSR by the foreign firm is beneficial to the domestic consumer, the protective tariff rate is not needed; the domestic government shall lower the tariff in order to increase the output of the foreign firm. A foreign firm's consumer-oriented CSR initiative makes it more aggressive in increasing the quantity of its export which will create a new "consumer surplus effect."

(4) YN, $\alpha_i = \alpha$ and $\alpha_j = 0$, then

$$t^{YN} = \frac{a(14+5(\alpha-3)\alpha)}{41+\alpha(5\alpha-26)};\ O_i^{YN} = \frac{2a^2(6-\alpha)(18+5(\alpha-4)\alpha)}{(41+\alpha(5\alpha-26))^2} - K$$

$$O_j^{YN} = \frac{3a^2(5-3\alpha)^2}{2(41+\alpha(5\alpha-26))^2};\ CS^{YN} = \frac{a^2(17-5\alpha)^2}{2(41+\alpha(5\alpha-26))^2}$$

$$SW^{YN} = \frac{a^2(21-10\alpha)}{82+2\alpha(5\alpha-26)} - K$$

$$GW^{YN} = \frac{a^2(21-10\alpha)}{82+2\alpha(5\alpha-26)} + \frac{3a^2(5-3\alpha)^2}{2(41+\alpha(5\alpha-26))^2} - K$$

Taking differentiation of t^{YN} with respect to α, we obtain:

$$\frac{\partial t^{YN}}{\partial \alpha} = \frac{a(5(54-11\alpha)\alpha-251)}{(41+\alpha(-26+5\alpha))^2} > 0, \text{ if } \alpha > \frac{1}{55}(135 - 2\sqrt{1105}).$$

***Lemma* 3.** *The unilateral adoption of the CSR strategy by the domestic firm makes it more aggressive on output decision and the government should raise the tariff rate imposing on the foreign product if the weight of consumer-friendly initiative is relatively high.*

If only domestic firm launches the CSR initiative and the weight is high initially, the rent-shifting effect coupled with the consumer surplus effect will change the equilibrium outcomes dramatically. Accordingly, the domestic government shall raise the import tariffs.

From the above 3 lemmas, we have the following proposition.

Proposition 1. *In an international duopolistic market, the consumer-oriented CSR initiatives will lower the tariff rate if the weight is relatively high in both cases of dual CSR and unilateral CSR by the foreign firm. The consumer-oriented CSR initiatives will raise the tariff rate if the weight is relatively high in the case of unilateral CSR by the domestic firm.*

In table 1, we present the payoff matrix in an international duopolistic game, where the equilibrium values of payoffs for the firms are summarized in Case (1)-(4).

Table 1. Payoffs to the Firms

		Foreign firm	
		Without CSR	With CSR
Home firm	Without CSR	O_i^{NN}, O_j^{NN}	O_i^{NY}, O_j^{NY}
	With CSR	O_i^{YN}, O_j^{YN}	O_i^{YY}, O_j^{YY}

We have the following proposition.

Proposition 2: *In an international duopolistic market, the consumer-oriented CSR initiative of both firms is the dominant strategy if the CSR cost is sufficiently low.*

Proof: We show that:

$$O_i^{YY} - O_i^{NY} \geq 0,$$
$$\text{if } K \leq \overline{K}_i \equiv \frac{1}{2}\alpha^2\left(\frac{(4-\alpha)(3-\alpha)(36+\alpha(-55+17\alpha))}{(41+\alpha(-38+9\alpha))^2} - \frac{3(12-5\alpha)^2}{(41-12\alpha)^2}\right),$$

$$O_j^{YY} - O_j^{YN} \geq 0,$$
$$\text{if } K \leq \overline{K}_j \equiv \frac{1}{2}\alpha^2\left(\frac{(5-\alpha^2)(15+\alpha(-34+11\alpha))}{(41+\alpha(-38+9\alpha))^2} - \frac{3(5-3\alpha)^2}{(41+\alpha(-26+5\alpha))^2}\right).$$

Hence, when $K \leq \min[\overline{K}_i, \overline{K}_j]$, (O_i^{YY}, O_j^{YY}) is the dominant strategy.

If the weight of consumer-friendly initiative is sufficient high, the weight assigned on CSR will lower the optimal tariff rate of the home country, and the profit of both firms will increase if the cost of CSR is sufficiently small.

Next, we consider the domestic social and global social welfare. We have the following proposition.

Proposition 3: *In an international duopolistic market, the consumer-oriented CSR initiative of both firms is the domestic social welfare optimum if the CSR cost is sufficiently low and the weight of consumer-friendly initiative assigned to the objective function in the decision-making process is positive.*

Proof: We show that:

(i) $SW^{YY} - SW^{NY} = \frac{a^2\alpha(\alpha(121+\alpha(9\alpha-44))-136)}{2(12\alpha-41)(41+\alpha(9\alpha-38))} - K > 0$,

$if\, K < K_i^{s0} \equiv \frac{a^2\alpha(\alpha(121+\alpha(9\alpha-44))-136)}{2(12\alpha-41)(41+\alpha(9\alpha-38))}$.

(ii) $SW^{YY} - SW^{YN} = \frac{a^2\alpha(170+\alpha(\alpha(4+5\alpha)-111))}{2(41+\alpha(5\alpha-26))(41+\alpha(9\alpha-38))} > 0$, $if\, \alpha > 0$,

(iii) $SW^{YY} - SW^{NN} = \frac{a^2(153-74\alpha)\alpha}{41(41+\alpha(9\alpha-38))} - K > 0$,

$if\, K < K_i^{s1} \equiv \frac{a^2(153-74\alpha)\alpha}{41(41+\alpha(9\alpha-38))}$.

From (i), (ii) and (iii), we have SW^{YY} is superior than other status, if $K \leq min.[K_i^{s0}, K_i^{s1}]$ and $\alpha > 0$.

It is clear that the dual adoption of the CSR strategy by the both firms makes them more aggressive on output decision; the consumer's surplus will increase. In addition, the consumer-oriented CSR initiative of both firms is the dominant strategy if the CSR cost is sufficiently low. The dual adoption of the CSR strategy will then make the global social welfare even higher and the lower import tariff will be the welfare-improving policy.

Proposition 4: *In an international duopolistic market, the consumer-oriented CSR initiative of both firms is the global social welfare optimum if the CSR cost is sufficiently low.*

Proof: We show that:

(i) $GW^{YY} - GW^{NY} > 0$, if

$$K < K_i^{g0} \equiv \frac{a^2(\alpha(478183+\alpha(+\alpha(237604+\alpha(3\alpha(345\alpha-871)-38524))-523998))-126075)}{(41-12\alpha)^2(41+\alpha(9\alpha-38))^2}$$

(ii) $GW^{YY} - GW^{YN} > 0$, if

$$K < K_j^{g1} \equiv \frac{a^2(\alpha(558215+\alpha(\alpha(563793+\alpha(\alpha(13937+\alpha(9359+25\alpha(10\alpha-113)))-186319)-816639)))-126075)}{(41+\alpha(5\alpha-26))^2(41+\alpha(9\alpha-38))^2}$$

(iii) $GW^{YY} - GW^{NN} > 0$, if

$$K < K_j^{g2} \equiv \frac{a^2(\alpha(516928+\alpha(2(84411-10549\alpha)\alpha-478213))-126075)}{1681(41+\alpha(9\alpha-38))^2}.$$

From (i), (ii) and (iii), we have GW^{YY} which is superior to other scenarios, if $K \leq min.[K_i^{g0}, K_j^{g1}, K_j^{g2}]$.

Moreover, the dual adoption of the CSR strategy is optimum for the global social welfare.

CONCLUSION

In an international duopolistic market, we showed that the consumer-oriented CSR initiatives will make the domestic government lower the tariff rate if the weight is relatively high in both cases of dual CSR and unilateral CSR by the foreign firm; however, the government will raise the tariff rate if the weight is relatively high in the case of unilateral CSR by the domestic firm.

Furthermore, the consumer-oriented CSR initiative of both firms is the dominant strategy if the CSR cost is sufficiently low. More importantly, the consumer-oriented CSR initiative of both firms is the global social welfare optimum if the CSR cost is sufficiently low coupled with trade liberalization.

REFERENCES

Bagnoli, M. and S. G. Watts. (2003). "Selling to Socially Responsible Consumers: Competition and the Private Provision of Public Goods," *Journal of Economics and Management Strategy 12*, 419-445.

Baron, D. P. (2001). "Private Politics, Corporate Social Responsibility and Integrated Strategy," *Journal of Economics and Management Strategy* 10, 7-45.

Baron D. P. (2009). "A Positive Theory of Moral Management, Social Pressure, and Corporate Social Performance," *Journal of Economics and Manage Strategy 18*, 7-43.

Bénabou, R. and J. Tirole. (2010). "Individual and Corporate Social Responsibility," *Economica,* 77 1-19.

Besley, T. and M. Ghatak. (2007). "Retailing Public Goods: The Economics of Corporate Social Responsibility," *Journal of Public Economics,* 91 1645-1663.

Chang, Y.-M., H.-Y. Chen, L. F. S. Wang and S.-J. Wu (2014). "Corporate Social Responsibility and International Competition: A Welfare Analysis," *Review of International Economics* 22, 625-638.

Kotchen, M. J. (2006). "Green Markets and Provision of Public Goods," *Journal of Political Economy* 114, 816-834.

Liu, C.-C., L. F. S. Wang and S.-H. Lee. (2015). "Strategic Environmental Corporate Social Responsibility in a Differentiated Duopoly Market," *Economics Letters* 129 108-111.

Manasakis, C., E. Mitrokostas and E. Petrakis. (2013). "Certification of Corporate Social Responsibility Activities in Oligopolistic Markets," *Canadian Journal of Economics*, 46 282-309.

Porter, M. E. and M. R. Kramer. (2006). "Strategy and Society: The Link between Competitive Advantage and Corporate Social Responsibility," *Harvard Business Review*, 84, 78-92.

Wang, L. F. S., Y. C. Wang and L. Zhao. (2012). "Tariff Policy and Welfare in an International Duopoly with Consumer-friendly Initiative," *Bulletin of Economic Research,* 64, 56-64.

Wood, D. J. (1991). "Corporate Social Performance Revisited," *Academy of Management Review 18*, 691-718.

In: Trade Liberalization
Editor: Pauline Santos
ISBN: 978-1-63483-867-2

Chapter 3

THE STATE AS A DETERMINANT OF THE PATTERN OF AGRICULTURAL TRADE

Wanki Moon[1,*], Hyeon Joon Shin[2] and Gabriel Pino[3]
[1]Department of Agribusiness Economics,
Southern Illinois University, Carbondale, IL, US
[2]Falls School of Business, Anderson University, Anderson, IN, US
[3]Facultad de Economía y Negocios,
Universidad de Talca, Talca, Chile

ABSTRACT

This chapter attempts to shed light on the role of the state in determining international competitiveness of agricultural commodities (unprocessed) and the pattern of agricultural trade. Farmers are neither the ones who make decisions whether or not to enter international markets nor are the ones who invest in R&D and attempt to develop new technologies with the goal of enhancing international competitiveness. Liberalizing trade is likely to send signals first to trading corporations, grain handlers, and governments and transmitted to farmers indirectly. Freer trade would initiate the process of specialization of production across the world, generating benefits in terms of greater production and lower prices, but offering little additional incentive for individual farm producers to reduce costs or adopt new technologies for the purpose of enhancing export opportunities (hence, lacking the creative destruction

* Corresponding author: wmoon@siu.edu.

processes like in the manufacturing sector in which firm level strategies would determine international competitiveness). However, states may compete with each other to expand their exports or to decrease their dependence on food imports with strategic investments in agricultural infrastructure. The point is that state level strategies will determine the pattern of agricultural trade in the long run. The implication for low-income/food insecure developing countries is that the state should play a proactive role in advancing agricultural development and making investment decisions for building agricultural production capacity (through public investments in R&D and extension services) and constructing/fostering the markets for agricultural inputs (credits, risks, information, transportation, managerial).

Keywords: agricultural trade, the state, the market, the Post-Washington Consensus

INTRODUCTION

The role of the state in shaping an economy is a topic of perennial controversy in economics and other social sciences. In neoclassical economics, the state is supposed to provide an institutional framework for protecting private property rights and correct market failures (externalities, public goods, and imperfect competition). Neoclassical economics renders the market the most prominent institution in charge of allocating scarce resources in an economy with the state and the firm playing a supporting role. The efficiency of an economy would be maximized in neoclassical economics when the state does little else, given that the market has a self-regulating mechanism. Political economy, however, postulates that the state is an active actor in determining market/economic outcomes and considers interactions between the state and the market as a notable sphere to study. The field of International Political Economy (IPE) poses various theories (world views) including liberalism, realism, Marxism, statism, nationalism, and mercantilism and permits varying interpretations of the state. While the individual consumer/firm is the unit of analysis for inquiries in the liberal tradition (classical economics, neoclassical economics, neoliberalism), the state is the formal unit of analysis for other IPE theories, hence playing a key role in determining interstate economic relations.

In general, the liberal theory posits that the state is an unprejudiced organization coordinating conflicts across diverse interest groups guided by impersonal market forces and always achieving harmonious results. The libertarian theory (public choice school) posits that the state consists of politicians and bureaucrats who have agendas in support of their own interests rather than the interests of voters or national interests. The Marxists postulates that the state serves the interests of the capitalists. In development theories, the state may be an authoritarian developmental state dedicated to accelerating industrialization and modernization in a developing country so as to catch up with advanced economies. Positive political economy poses the state as an institution designed to coordinate conflicts among various interest groups given constitutions and laws within the state. According to this view, the state may or may not have its own agenda or autonomy, but it is an organic entity influenced by various forces within its political/economic system. Differing from the liberal view, the positive political economy approach clearly recognizes conflictual (rather than harmonious) relationships among various groups, which may not be easily coordinated by market forces therefore creating room for politics to weigh in.

Given such diverse views of the state in theory, the purpose of this chapter is to probe the role of the state specifically in agricultural trade, one of the most contentious subject matters in contemporary international economic affairs. Over the last fifteen years, the World Trade Organization (WTO) has been endeavoring to liberalize agricultural trade through the Doha Round, however, with little success despite the solid framework laid by the Uruguay Round Agreement on Agriculture (URAA). Some researchers call the task of liberalizing agricultural trade a wicked problem that is inherently complicated. There would be no straightforward solutions for such a wicked problem. There are proponents and opponents of trade liberalization in agriculture. Proponents argue that trade liberalization in agriculture will benefit the global economy by stimulating specialization of agricultural production across the world and results in substantial increases in national incomes and welfare for all countries involved. Opponents counter that international markets in agriculture are already severely distorted due to agricultural protection in developed countries in the postwar period, which has strengthened their agricultural sector considerably and turning many of them into agricultural exporters and liberalizing is likely to fixate such distortions and deprive food insecure developing countries of the opportunities to advance their agricultural development. Proponents argue that states should stay out of the international flow of agricultural products, while opponents believing that states should play an important role in developing the agricultural sector, especially in developing and least developed countries and therefore should have the flexibility to manage international trade in agriculture.

The chapter is organized as follows. The next two sections introduces trade-related theories and debates in an effort to illustrate the role of the state in economic growth/development and in conserving the environment conceptually and empirically. In particular, the debates on the Washington Consensus vs Post-Washington Consensus are described. The fourth section analyzes agricultural trade in detail and examines whether there are differences between the agricultural and manufacturing sectors in terms of the role of the state. It discusses the implications of the differences between the two sectors in terms of what benefits of trade are realized. The last section provides concluding remarks.

ECONOMIC THEORIES OF INTERNATIONAL TRADE

The early theoretical insight supporting free trade originates from the notion of gains from trade associated with classical political economists such as Adam Smith and David Ricardo in the 18th and 19th century. Smith argues in his book "The Wealth of Nations" that international trade is beneficial to all nations:

> The importation of gold and silver is not the principal, much less the sole benefit which a nation derives from its foreign trade. Between whatever places foreign trade is carried on, they all of them derive two distinct benefits from it. It carries out that surplus part of the produce of their land and labour for which there is no demand among them, and brings back in return for it something else for which there is a demand. It gives a value to their superfluities, by exchanging them for something else, which may satisfy a part of their wants, and increase their enjoyments. By means of it the narrowness of the home market does not hinder the division of labour in any particular branch of art or manufacture from being carried to the highest perfection. By opening a more extensive market for whatever part of the produce of their labour may exceed the home consumption, it encourages them to improve its productive powers, and to augment its annual produce to the utmost, and thereby to increase the real revenue and wealth of the society. (IV. 1.31) [1]

Smith believes that a country's trade is mainly driven by the gap between its sectoral supply and demand levels: i.e., a country exports goods and

[1] Smith(reprinted, 1996).

services that it produces most efficiently and imports those that other countries produce more efficiently, thereby maximizing its wealth. Known as the theory of absolute advantage, Smith's idea raises a question whether international trade is irrelevant when a country can produce all goods more efficiently than other countries (i.e., has absolute advantage in all goods involved).

Offering a seamless answer for the question, David Ricardo strengthened the rationale for free trade in a pathbreaking way by developing the concept of comparative advantage and demonstrated that trade generates gains for both exporting and importing countries even when the exporting (importing) country has absolute (dis) advantages in all the goods traded. The Ricardian comparative advantage or disadvantage would arise whenever there are differences in production technology (e.g., labor productivity) among countries. The ideas of Adam Smith and David Ricardo constitute the intellectual foundation of economic liberalism of the 19th century and neoliberalism of the late 20th century. Two Swedish economists, Eli Heckscher and Bertil Ohlin refined the classical theory of trade by underscoring the role of the differences in production factor endowments in determining the pattern of trade. The Heckscher-Ohlin theory suggests that nations would benefit from specializing in the production of goods using their most abundant factor of production.

The benefits of freeing trade are realized *via* two mechanisms: (i) gains from specialization and (ii) enhancement in production efficiency. Gains from specialization arise when countries allocate scarce resources to sectors with comparative advantage, and the literature demonstrates that such gains exist under fairly general circumstances except for cases involving risky economies without markets for risks (Dixit and Norman 1980; Acemouglu and Ventura 2002; Bernhofen and Brown 2005).[2] Production efficiency is measured by total factor productivity (TFP) and increases in TFP have been shown to come from technology diffusion, competition promotion, and increases in R&D investment (Easterly and Levine 2001; Hall and Jones 1999; Keller 2000, 2004, Kim 2000; Ferreira and Rossi 2003; Grossman and Helpman 1991; Aghion et al. 2001). The benefits of the two mechanisms would manifest in the forms of lower prices, larger quantities, and greater varieties to consumers around the world, and expansion of the global economy, insofar as the sustainability of environmental and ecological resources is ensured by binding

[2] For example, see Krugman (1981) for intra-industry specialization, Markusen (1981) for imperfect competition, Markusen (1984) for multinationals and multi-point economies, and Dixit and Norman (1984) for trade without lump-sum compensation.

global rules. As such, the classical theory of trade depicts a harmonious global economy coordinated by the invisible hand at the global level.

In opposition to the mainstream economic theory of trade, Friedrich List (the founder of the German historical school of economics) presented in the late 19th century a differing view on the usefulness of free trade in growing national wealth. Specifically, he advanced infant industry protection as a logical argument why late-industrializing German businesses should be protected against competition from more advanced British manufacturers. The notion of the infant industry protection has been first used and practiced in 1791 by Alexander Hamilton, the Secretary of Treasury of the United States, who formulated trade policies to protect US industries in their infancy against imports from advanced British manufacturers. Analytically more elaborate critics on the mainstream thinking of trade emerged from within itself in the 1970s. Despite the prediction of the classical theory that there would be large trade flows across countries with different technologies and factor endowments and small trade flows between similar countries, empirical trade data shows that trade volume between countries with similar technologies and factor endowments is also large and the majority of trade flows is not across industries but within industries (Grubel and Lloyd 1975). This disparity between the classical trade theory and the real world observations gave birth to the new trade theory, which identified features like increasing returns of scale, imperfectly competitive industries, product differentiation, and externalities as potential causes of international trade in addition to differences in technology, factor endowments, and tastes (Krugman 1979, 1980; Helpman and Krugman 1985). The new trade theory establishes that the presence of such features presents an opportunity for a country to use trade policies (import restrictions or export subsidies) and increase its welfare level, thereby contradicting the preaching of the classical trade theory that any kinds of trade intervention are welfare-reducing.

THE WASHINGTON CONSENSUS VS. THE POST-WASHINGTON CONSENSUS

The divergence in thinking about the roles of the state and free trade in economic development between the mainstream and dissenting schools is well illustrated in the controversy surrounding the so called "Washington consensus (WS)." The WS refers to a set of guidelines for developing countries' policy reforms centered around macroeconomic stabilization, liberalization for trade and investment, privatization of state enterprises, and deregulation (Williams 1990). The WS policies were practiced in the 1980s and 1990s by the Washington-based international financial institutions (World Bank and IMF) and the US Treasury in the name of the structural adjustments program as a conditionality associated with the offering of foreign aids to developing countries. The consensus policies were rooted in a firm belief in unfettered markets and the minimal role of government in protecting property rights and enforcing contracts. The Washington consensus was deeply influenced by the neoliberal thinking that was fostered intellectually by Milton Friedman and Friedrich Hayek, and promoted politically by Ronald Reagan and Margaret Thatcher. Neoliberalism was in enthusiastic support of the Washington consensus policies as a development model alternative to Keynesianism and national developmentalism associated with the structuralist development thinking.

It is widely shared, however, that the Washington consensus policies have failed in moving forward the economies of the developing world (Gore 2000; Rodrik 2006; Stiglitz 2008; Birdsall, de la Torre, and Caicedo 2010). Indeed, they contributed to the Mexico crisis, the East Asian crises, the Russian crisis, and the Argentine crisis and left many developing countries (particularly in Sub-Saharan Africa and Latin America) going backward in terms of per capita income. The failure compelled some researchers to view the Washington consensus policies as like "kicking away the ladder," a phrase that List coined in his book (entitled *The National System of Political Economy* published in 1841) to portray the behavior of Great Britain preaching to other countries (including Germany) to liberalize their economies only after it had gained comparative advantage in the manufacturing sector in the 19th century in part as a consequence of protecting it for long since the 15th century (List 1841; Athukorala 2011). In particular, showing historically how now-developed countries including the US and Great Britain used a variety of protectionist policies during the early stages of their economic development to promote their own infant industries against imports from more advanced countries, Chang (2002) revived the same phrase in his book (entitled *Kicking Away the Ladder*) to highlight the gravity of allowing the policy space for developing countries to use tariffs, subsidies, public investment, and export promotion as an alternative development strategy to the Washington consensus. For List, Chang, and others advocating infant industry protection policies and other judicious government actions, the developed world's preaching of free trade and *laissez-faire* to developing countries is like covering up the protectionist policies that have worked very well for themselves.

The flaws of the Washington consensus policies became even more evident when contrasted with the success of East Asian countries including Korea and Taiwan during the periods between the 1960s and 1990s. While relying on outward-looking development policies focused on export promotion, the governments of the East Asian countries were engaged in a broad array of government interventions ranging from import restrictions (tariffs and qualitative barriers), export subsidies, industrial policies, and control of the allocation of financial capital. The export-oriented strategy was a development thinking seemingly in stark contrast with the import substitution industrialization (ISI) strategy that was adopted by many countries in Latin America between 1960s and 1980s. The ISI strategy was carved out from the neo-Marxist tradition (particularly the neo-structuralists' conceptions of international relations as reflected in the dependency theory that divides the world into two groups of countries: core industrialized countries in the North and underdeveloped periphery countries in the South. Since the periphery countries are destined to undergo the vicious cycle of the development of underdevelopment given the permanent structural constraints of exploitative relationship between the core and periphery countries that have been solidified through colonial and imperial periods for many centuries, the ISI strategy contends that the developing world should protect domestic industries and continually substitute imports until it becomes fully industrialized, hence called "inward-looking development strategy."

The sluggish performance of the ISI strategy in the 1960s and 1970s provided a good reason for Latin American countries to embrace the neoliberal Washington consensus policies. When contrasted with the ISI strategy, the export-oriented strategy is clearly more open and outward-looking, and therefore international financial institutions and liberal economists used to pick the East Asian countries as a triumphant story of the free trade doctrine and economic liberalism. Yet, they were hesitant to acknowledge the fact that the state has played a proactive role in the region in guiding/managing the systemic process of economic development (while remaining authoritarian politically); in provisioning the infrastructure needed for markets to grow to function well; and in cultivating dynamic comparative advantages for selected industries. Learning from the experiences of Korea and Taiwan, other Asian countries including China and Viet Nam followed the East Asian development model and have exhibited remarkable performances in growing their GDP. Such countries' development paths are formally referred to as the so called (authoritarian) 'developmental state' in the literature and recognized as a distinctive model of development appropriate for certain developing countries aspiring to catch up with the developed world.

In contrast with the Washington consensus relegating the role of the state to the mere provision of institutional frameworks for protecting private property rights and correcting market failures, the role of the state in the developmental state model is far-reaching encompassing the management of trade, risk sharing, control of capital outflows, selecting industries (picking winners) that would have the greatest spillover effects on the rest of the economy and subsidizing them. The experiences of the East Asian countries over the last decades show that the role of markets would expand in parallel with the growth of the economy. Imperfect markets would grow to be rectified and become more competitive by the entrance of new domestic or multinational firms. Further, political authorities would recognize the economic needs to create markets in areas like risks, information, or entrepreneurs that are typically absent in the early stage of economic development of a country. At the same time, the role of the state would begin to shift to other areas such as labor/capital market reforms, social safety net programs, environmental/ecological problems, and educational/technological development issues.

The failure of the Washington Consensus coupled with the rise of the developmental state (particularly the rise of China and India in the 1990s) brought about a revisionist thinking known as "the post-Washington Consensus," a term that Joseph Stiglitz used as the Senior Vice President for the World Bank while assessing the outcomes of the past development policies (Stiglitz 1998). The central point of the post-Washington consensus is that the WS relied too much on market fundamentalism, possibly carried away by the prevalence of neoliberalism as a policy paradigm since the 1980s. The post-Washington consensus indicates that there was a lack of understanding when markets work, when they do not work, and what are needed for markets to work. It is now increasingly recognized that markets are not naturally occurring or spontaneously functioning institution and therefore markets need to be supported with the infusion of such factors as competition, information, fair rules, trust, risk/uncertainty handling, and physical infrastructure (North 1994). In addition, critics indicate that the WS put too much trust on static comparative advantages rather than dynamic comparative advantage and took a too simplistic mantra that the state is the problem but not the solution and government failures are destined to impose greater harms than market failures. The post Washington consensus acknowledges that it takes time for markets to develop and function properly; there should be appropriate balance in the roles of the state and markets; and one-size-fits-all strategy does not work for all developing countries.

TRADE, THE ENVIRONMENT AND NATURAL RESOURCES

The above analysis suggests that the state has an important role to play in international trade and economic development especially for developing countries. Another area of controversy about the role of the state centers on the effects of trade on the environment and the sustainability of renewable natural resources. The debate over whether freer trade is better or worse for the environment began in earnest when environmental degradations (global warming and industrial pollution) emerged as an important issue in the trade negotiations during the North American Free Trade Agreement (NAFTA) and the Uruguay Round of GATT in the early 1990s. The literature is grouped into two broad categories: i) the effects of trade on the degradation of environmental quality, and ii) the effects of trade on the conservation of natural resources.

The academic debate over the link between international trade and the degradation of environmental quality has revolved around two controversial hypothesis: the "Environmental Kuznets Curve hypothesis (EKC)[3]" and the "pollution haven hypothesis (DHH).[4]" The EKC is a hypothesized, inverted U-shaped relationship between income per capita and pollution emissions. According to the EKC, pollution in the environmental Kuznets curve rapidly grows as income per capita rises in the early stage of economic growth, because people are more interested in growth rather than clean air and water and they are still too poor to pay for environmental protection. The EKC also predicts that, as per capita income continues to rise beyond its threshold, pollution begins to fall along the curve (Dasgupta et al. 2002; Dinda 2004; Stern 2004). Based upon the EKC, neoclassical economists argue that income growth brought about by trade positively affects the environment in two ways: increasing the demand for better environmental quality and increasing the government's ability to invest in environmental protection (Grossman and Krueger 1993; Dasgupta et al. 2002). Much of the empirical literature on the

---

[3] Kuznets's name was attached to the curve by Grossman and Krueger (1993) who noted its resemblance to Kuznets's inverted-U relationship between income inequality and development.

[4] It is also called the "Dirty Industry Migration Hypothesis."

EKC leads us to be skeptical about its existence and significance. In various theoretical settings, a couple of early studies, such as Lopez (1994) and Selden and Song (1995), obtained an inverted U-shaped relationship between income level and some pollutants. But, Stern (1998, 2004) argues that the evidence for the inverted U-shaped relationship applies only to local pollutants, not to global pollutants. For example, Stern et al. (2001) empirically find that sulfur emissions per capita show an inverted U-shaped relationship with income per capital only in high-income countries, but they are globally a monotonic function of income per capita. Even though the EKC exists, the turning points for pollutants are often estimated to be at too high income levels for developing countries to achieve (Stern et al. 1996, 2001).

The PHH claims that lax environmental regulations in developing countries provide them with a comparative advantage in more pollution-intensive production. According to the PHH, therefore, free trade relocates pollution-intensive industries from developed countries to developing countries. If the PHH holds, the existence of the EKC partly implies that developed countries has solved their environmental problems by relocating dirty industries to developing countries. Much literature has examined the validity of the PHH and generated mixed findings. Jaffe et al. (1995) and Janicke et al. (1997) find no empirical support for the PHH. Further, the former also finds that the costs of abatement are not a significant factor in industrial relocation from the North to the South. But, Birdsall and Wheeler (1993) and Lucas et al. (1992) finds significant evidence for displacements of pollution-intensive industries to developing countries, even though it is not explained by differences in environmental regulation between the North and the South. Using detailed data on North–South trade flows for pollution intensive products, Cole (2004) also finds supporting evidence for the PHH. Antweiler et al. (2001) examine three different channels through which free trade may affect sulfur dioxide emissions: the scale effect (trade lead to more economic activity and thus higher pollution), the technique effect (trade leads to higher income, thus cleaner production technique and lower pollution), and the composition effect (in developing countries, trade alters the industrial composition toward pollution-intensive industries). They conclude that free trade is good for the environment, because the technique effect dominates the other effects. Ecological economists refute the neoclassical conceptualization of trade and its virtuous effect on the environment, and they suggests new paradigms of international trade predicated on the principle of environmental justice and sustainability (Daly and Goodland 1994; Ekins et al. 1994;

Muradian and Martinex-Alier 2001; Ropke 1994; Seidl and Tisdell 1999; Tisdell 2001).

The impact of trade liberalization on renewable resources[5] is very difficult to measure, mostly because of the dynamics of renewable resources that are determined by interactions between economic, ecological/biological and institutional variables. The economics literature on this topic, therefore, has focused on the roles of various factors in the link between trade liberalization and renewable resource. Trade liberalization primarily affects open-access renewable resources through changing their prices relative to the prices of other goods. In a small, closed economy, for example, when it is closed, the price of its abundant natural resource is simply the domestic equilibrium price. But, with openness to trade, the price is set in the world market, and this economy has to take the world price as given. The long-run effect of trade depends on whether it raises or lowers the domestic price. Brander and Taylor (1997a) show that a higher world price of logs usually encourages small, forest-abundant countries to overexploit their forest, thereby causing their stocks to decline faster. Thus, unless forests are well-managed, trade liberalization may be welfare-reducing in the long-run for small timber-exporting countries, even though there are initial gains from trade. The problem of overexploitation may be worse for large resource-exporting countries (Brander and Taylor 1998). Changing relative prices also indirectly affects open-access renewable resources by adjusting the amount of habitats for them. Jinji (2006) extends the Brander and Taylor (1997) model by endogenizing the carrying capacity of forests and theoretically finds that trade liberalization rather raises timber stocks in small, forest-abundant countries. This finding means that a higher timber price does not only lead to overexploitation but also gives them more incentive to maintain and expand their forests. In the study of Lopez (2000), in contrast, trade liberalization may cause a significant improvement in agricultural productivity, thus leading to deforestation. In the case of Côte d'Ivoire, the author finds out that higher agricultural productivity after trade liberalization causes forests to be converted for agricultural uses. Barbier (2001) and Smulders et al. (2004) also warn that trade restrictions reduces a small, timber-exporting country's terms of trade, thus negatively affecting its forest conservation.

In summary, the efficacy of institutions managing natural resources matters a great deal in the results of the studies reviewed above. Weak

---

[5] Renewable resources are organic natural resources, such as fisheries, forests, wildlife and the benefits provided by ecosystems and biodiversity, which can replenish to overcome usage and consumption (Fischer 2010).

institutions and lax regulations in resource-abundant developing countries may lead to the tragedy of the commons, and trade liberalization may cause them to export their abundant natural resources and thus overexploit them. Brander and Taylor (1997b) consider trade between a consumer country and a conservationist country [6] and theoretically find that trade liberalization gives the consumer country a comparative advantage in exporting its renewable resources and causes it to deplete them, thus leading it to long-run welfare losses from trade. The upshot is that stronger institutions lead to improvements in the conservation of renewable resources, pointing to the state as important in using renewable natural resources in a sustainable manner.

THE STATE AS A DETERMINANT OF THE PATTERN OF AGRICULTURAL TRADE

The preceding discussion shows that, while free trade offers a number of mechanisms through which net economic benefits are generated for all states involved, there are considerable room for states to use protectionist trade policies and increase their national wealth/welfare, while conserving the environment and natural resources. It should be fair to state that free trade is not a universal policy guidance that is applicable to every case regardless of space/time and the type of industries involved. This section presents an analysis of what role the state plays in determining international competitiveness of agricultural commodities and the pattern of agricultural trade, particularly when compared to the manufacturing sector.

Before probing the role of the state in agricultural trade in depth, it is needed to clarify two issues of analytic importance. The first issue concerns the question of what is the unit of analysis when researching agricultural trade. The economic theory of trade postulates that states trade with each other (i.e., national governments make international transactions with each other), indicating that the unit of analysis of international trade is the state. In practice, international trade, however, involves economic transactions between private firms (importers and exporters) in different countries, although state trading represents one form of international trade in the agricultural sector at the present time. The second issue is about what commodities/products are

[6] In Brander and Taylor (1997b), a consumer country is defined as a country with open access to its natural resource pool, whereas a conservationist country has a restricted access to its natural resources in order to conserve them.

included in agricultural trade. While agricultural trade in general encompasses both raw food and nonfood commodities and processed/manufactured food products, the analysis in this chapter identifies agricultural trade in a narrower scope that incorporates international trade only in raw unprocessed agricultural commodities with a particular focus on grains/oilseeds (rice, wheat, corn, soybean, barley, oats, rye, feed grains, coarse grains such as millet and sorghum). Processed/manufactured food products would then belong to the manufacturing sector.

Agricultural Sector vs. Manufacturing Sector in International Trade

With the two caveats in mind, we examine below how the agricultural and manufacturing sectors differ regarding two questions of importance in analyzing the effects of international trade and trade liberalization: (i) who makes decisions about the international transactions and (ii) what determines international competitiveness of the products traded.[7] In the case of the trading of manufactured goods, it is the private business firms that would identify markets; decide whether or not to enter international markets depending on the international competitiveness of their products; and perform all transactions needed for exporting their products. Firm level strategies (e.g., investment, R&D) are therefore important in determining the trade patterns of the manufacturing sector in addition to natural comparative advantages inherent at the state level.

In the case of the agricultural sector, agricultural commodities (e.g., grains, oilseeds, feed grains) are produced by farmers, assembled by grain handlers or cooperatives, and exported internationally by trading firms, which are large multinational corporations controlling procuring, selling, financing, and delivering to importing firms or state trading agencies around the world. That is, farmers are neither the ones who make decisions whether or not to enter international markets nor are the ones who invest in R&D and attempt to develop new technologies. Agricultural production efficiency/technology is determined by public investments in agricultural technology, extension

[7] The term international competitiveness is used differently from comparative advantage. While comparative advantage is a concept defined at the country level, international competitiveness is defined at the firm level, indicating that, depending on the effectiveness of long-term strategies, individual firms may be able to overcome comparative disadvantages and export their products to foreign countries.

services, and rural/farming infrastructure. [8] Farm producers simply decide whether or not to adopt new technologies. Strategies and public policies at the state level are therefore pertinent in determining the pattern of agricultural trade in addition to natural comparative advantage.

In short, international competitiveness is determined basically at the firm level for the manufacturing sector (assuming that institutional and technological environments at the state level remain constant) and at the state level for the agricultural sector. Reducing barriers to trade in the manufacturing sector are likely to open up exporting opportunities for a greater number of firms around the world, thereby promoting competition in international markets and compelling them to become more lean and better organized; reduce costs; improve the quality of their products; adopt new technologies; or invest in R&D to develop new technologies so as to outcompete rivals, secure greater market shares, and earn higher profits. The added competition among firms in international markets would benefit consumers around the world with potentially lower prices, higher quality of products, and/or greater varieties of products. The role of the state is merely to ensure that the firms follow environmental and labor regulations that would meet international standards.

For the agricultural sector, the state matters a great deal in determining the effects of trade liberalization. Reducing barriers to trade in the agricultural sector will first send signals to trading corporations, grain handlers, and governments. Then, the signals will be transmitted to farmers through market and nonmarket (e.g., public extension services) channels. Based on the indirect (transmitted) signals, farmers may or may not alter their decisions regarding what to produce (crop mixes), how much (acreages), and how (technology adoption). In countries with comparative advantage in agricultural production (natural resource endowments favorable to agriculture), farmers are likely to receive signals to expand their production; and farmers in countries with comparative disadvantage in agricultural production would receive signals to reduce their production. The adjustments in production between countries based on natural comparative advantages would foster a specialized system of agricultural production at the global scale. Yet, states' long-term strategic investment in agriculture (compatible with international trade rules) may promote technological innovations, reduce costs or improve productivity,

[8] In addition, input supply business firms (seed; machine; fertilizers; herbicides; pesticides) are in a position to influence agricultural production technology. In theory, if the input supply firms operate globally, farm producers around the world should have equal access to new technologies provided by the input supply firms.

potentially enhancing international competitiveness of their agricultural commodities, or reducing the need for imports or producing surpluses and exporting them. Hence, the entities attempting to develop newer technologies are not farm producers but national governments (and input supply business corporations).

The point is that whereas individual firms are in a position to determine their competitiveness in the manufacturing sector, it is the state that plays the remaining role in determining the competitiveness of agricultural raw commodities once the endowments of natural resources and initial labor productivity shapes natural comparative advantage and trade patterns.

Benefits of Freeing Trade in the Agricultural Sector vs Manufacturing Sector

This difference between the agricultural and manufacturing sectors has an important ramification in uncovering what types of benefits are realized when trade is liberalized. As noted earlier, the benefits of free trade occur through two mechanisms: gains from specialization (scarce resources are allocated more efficiently across the world) and dynamic improvements in production efficiency due to greater competition and new technology adoption/diffusion. While the manufacturing sector enjoys both benefits, the agricultural sector is not likely to experience dynamic improvements in production efficiency. Once international competitiveness of agricultural commodities is determined by comparative advantages at the state level, freer trade offers little additional incentive for individual farm producers to reduce costs or adopt new technologies (or farmers have no leverages available to them to improve their international competitiveness) for the purpose of enhancing export opportunities, although states may be motivated to invest more in improving agricultural infrastructure and promoting agricultural technologies.

Trade liberalization delivers benefits in the forms of lower prices, larger quantities, higher product quality, and greater varieties for the case of the manufacturing sector. For the agricultural sector, the initial process of specialization of production across different countries of the world kicked off by trade liberalization would lower prices and produce higher quantities in theory (in the real world, trade liberalization would initially increase the prices for the commodities that developed countries have subsidized consistently during the postwar period because there would be lower production without subsidies). However, given the passive role of farm producers in international trade and their lack of leverages to become more innovative (cost reducing; increasing yields) beyond the ones existing in domestic markets once a particular configuration of the specialization of agricultural production is established, then there are not likely to be much further benefit that may be realized through competition and subsequent creative destruction processes (entrepreneurial innovations) among firms, which are present in the case of the manufacturing sector.

CONCLUSION

This chapter shows that it is the state that would determine international competitiveness of agricultural commodities (unprocessed) and the pattern of agricultural trade once natural resources and factor endowments shape comparative advantage. That is in contrast to the manufacturing sector in which firm level strategies would determine international competitiveness of manufactured products. This difference implies that free trade in the manufacturing sector would bring about economic gains by promoting competition and creative destruction processes (entrepreneurial innovations) among firms. But there may be no such gains in the agricultural sector, because farmers do neither face greater competition nor undergo creative destruction processes among themselves once international competitiveness of agricultural commodities are determined by comparative advantages at the state level. That is, freer trade offers little additional incentive for individual farm producers to reduce costs or adopt new technologies (or farmers have no leverages available to them to improve their international competitiveness) for the purpose of enhancing export opportunities. Yet, when a state has the desire to become an exporter in some agricultural commodities or to strengthen domestic production capacity, it can craft long-term strategies; make investments in strengthening agricultural infrastructure or in developing new technologies; reduce costs; and produce commodities of higher quality, thereby potentially improving international competitiveness. Hence, what goals states have in relation to their agriculture would determine the international competitiveness of agricultural commodities and the pattern of agricultural trade in the long-term.

The implication of this study for developing or food insecure low income countries is that the state should play a proactive role in using agricultural trade as a strategy of advancing agricultural/economic development particularly in consideration of the strong evidence that agricultural growth is indispensable for overall economic growth (Gollin, Pabente, and Rogerson 2002; Tiffin and Irz 2006; Self and Grabowski 2007). The state should make major investments in the initial stages of economic development for building agricultural production capacity (through public investments in R&D and extension services) and constructing/fostering the markets for agricultural inputs (credits, risks, information, transportation, managerial). The directions suggested by policy paradigms such as laissez-faire, free trade, market fundamentalism, neoliberalism, or the Washington Consensus are not very well suited for agricultural development/markets (Moon 2011). Even agricultural production and markets in developed countries would not be able to maintain farm/rural economic stability or vitality without public actions (state interventions) in areas like dealing with uncertainty, risks, safety nets, infrastructure, technical assistance, information provision, and other extension services.

Advancing agricultural development in low income countries should be a steady and sustained process of building public institutions for provisioning physical infrastructure and assisting markets to rise and function well, which is exactly what developed countries have done to develop their agriculture. Markets are not self-rising, self-sustaining, or self-correcting especially for agricultural commodities. Market failures (imperfect markets or missing markets) arising in the process of agricultural development should not be left unaddressed because of the fear of government failures. Developing countries may experience government failures, but they would experience institutional learning, too. The successful experiences of the developmental state model in East Asia should prove to be a good example showing that such learning do indeed take place in practice.

REFERENCES

Acemoglu, Daron. & Jaume, Ventura. (2002). "The World Income Distribution." *Quarterly Journal of Economics* 117, 659-694.

Aghion, Philippe, Christopher Harris, Peter Howitt & John Vickers. (2001). "Competition, Imitation and Growth with Step-by-step Innovation." *Review of Economic Studies*, *68*, 467-492.

Antweiler, Werner., Brian, R. Copeland. & M. Scott Taylor. (2001). “Is Free Trade Good for the Environment?” *American Economic Review*, *91*, 877-908.

Athukorala, Prema-chandra. (2011). “Production Networks and Trade Patterns in East Asia: Regionalization or Globalization?” *Asian Economic Papers* 1*0*, 65-95

Barbier, Edward B. (2001). “International Trade and Sustainable Forestry.” In *International Environmental Economics: A Survey of the Issues*, by G. G. Schulze and H. W. Ursprung 114-147. Oxford: Oxford University Press.

Bernhofen, Daniel M. & John, C. Brown. (2005). “An Empirical Assessment of the Comparative Advantage Gains from Trade: Evidence from Japan.” *American Economic Review*, *95* 208-225.

Birdsall, Nancy & David Wheeler. (1993). “Trade Policy and Industrial Pollution in Latin America: Where Are the Pollution Haven?” *Journal of Environment and Development* 2 137-149.

Birdsall, Nancy., Augusto, de la Torre. & Felipe, Valencia Caicedo. (2010). “The Washington Consensus: Assessing a Damaged Brand.” Working Paper 211. Washington DC: Center for Global Development.

Brander, James A. & M. Scott Taylor. (1997a). “International Trade and Open-access Renewable Resources: The Small Open Economy Case.” *Canadian Journal of Economics*, *30*, 526-552.

—. (1997b). “International Trade Between Consumer and Consevationist's Countries.” *Resource and Energy Economics* 19 267-297.

—. (1998). “Open Access Renewable Resources: Trade and Trade Policy in a Two-Country Model.” *Journal of International Economics*, *44* 181-209.

Chang, Ha-joon. (2002). *Kicking Away the Ladder*. London, UK: Anthem Press.

Cole, Matthew A. (2004). “Trade, the Pollution Haven Hypothesis and the Environmental Kuznets Curve: Examining the Linkages.” *Ecological Economics*, *48*, 71-81.

Daly, Herman. & Robert, Goodland. (1994). “An Ecological-Economic Assessment of Deregulation of International Commerce under GATT.” *Ecological Economics*, *9*, 73-93.

Dasgupta, Susmita., Benoit, Laplante., Hua, Wang. & David, Wheeler. (2002). “Confronting the Environmental Kuznets Curve.” *Journal of Economic Perspectives* 16 147-168.

Dinda, Soumyananda. (2004). “Environmental Kuznets Curve Hypothesis: A Survey.” *Ecological Economics*, *49*, 431-455.

Dixit, Avinash, & Victor, Norman. (1986). "Gains from Trade without Lump-sum Compensation." *Journal of International Economics 21* 111-122.

—. (1980). *Theory of International Trade: A Dual, General Equilibrium Approach*. Cambridge, UK: Cambridge University Press.

Easterly, William, & Ross, Levine. (2001). "It's Not Factor Accumulation: Stylized Facts and Growth Model." *World Bank Economic Review* 15 177–219.

Ekins, Paul,, Carl, Folke, & Robert, Costanza. (1994). "Trade, Environment & Development: The Issues in Perspective." *Ecological Economics*, *9* 1-12.

Ferreira, Pedro C. & Jose L. Rossi. (2003). "New Evidence from Brazil on Trade Liberalization and Productivity Growth." *International Economic Review*, *44*, (1383) (1405).

Fischer, Carolyn. (2010). "Does Trade Help or Hinder the Conservation of Natural Resources?" *Review of Environmental Economics and Policy*, *4* 103-121.

Gollin, Douglas, Stephen Parente and Richard. Rogerson. (2002). "The Role of Agriculture in Development." *American Economic Review*, *92* 160-164.

Gore, Charles. (2000). "The Rise and Fall of the Washington Consensus as a Paradigm for Developing Countries." *World Development* 28, 780-804.

Grossman, Gene, & Anne, O. Krueger. (1993). "Environmental Impacts of the North American Free Trade Agreement." In *The U.S.-Mexico Free Trade Agreement*, by P Garber 13-56. Cambridge, MA: MIT Press.

Grossman, Gene, & Elhanan, Helpman. (1991). *Innovation and Growth in the Global Economy*. Cambridge, MA: MIT Press.

Grubel, Herbert G. & Peter J. Lloyd. (1975). *Intra-Industry Trade: The Theory and Management of International Trade in Differentiated Product*. London: Macmillan.

Hall, Robert, & Charles, Jones. (1999). "Why Do Some Countries Produce So Much More Output Per Worker Than Others?" *Quarterly Journal of Economics* 1*14*, 83-116.

Helpman, Elhanan. & Paul, R. Krugman. (1985). *Market Structure and Foreign Trade: Increasing Returns, Imperfect Competition, and the International Economy*. Cambridge, USA: MIT Press.

Jaffe, Adam B., Steven, R. Peterson. & Paul, R. Portney. (1995). "Environmental Regulation and the Competitiveness of U.S. Manufacturing: What Does the Evidence Tell Us?" *Journal of Economic Literature*, *33* 132-163.

Janicke, Martin., Manfred, Binder. & Harald, Monch. (1997). "'Dirty Industries': Patterns of Change in Industrial Countries." *Environmental and Resource Economics*, *9*, 467-491.

Jinji, Naoto. (2006). "International Trade and Terrestrial Open-access Renewable Resources in a Small Open Economy." *Canadian Journal of Economics*, *39*, 790-808.

Keller, Wolfgang. (2000). "Do Trade Patterns and Technology Flows Affect Productivity Growth?" *World Bank Economic Review* *14* 17-47.

Keller, Wolfgang. (2004). "International Technology Diffusion." *Journal of Economic Literature XLII*: 752-782.

Kim, Euysung. (2000). "Trade Liberalization and Productivity Growth in Korean Manufacturing Industries: Price Protection, Market Power and Scale Efficiency." *Journal of Development Economics*, *62*, 55-83.

Krugman, Paul R. (1979). "Increasing returns, monopolistic competition and international trade." *Journal of International Economics*, *9*, 469-479.

—. (1980). "Scale Economies, Product Differentiation and the Pattern of Trade." *American Economic Review*, *70*, 950-959.

—. (1981). "Intraindustry Specialization and the Gains from Trade." *Journal of Political Economy*, *89*, 959-973.

List, F. (1841). *The National System of Political Economy (English Edition, (1904))*. London, UK: Longman.

Lopez, Ramon. (1994). "The Environment as a Factor of Production: The Effect of Economic Growth and Trade Liberalization." *Journal of Environmental Economics and Management* 27 163-184.

—. (2000). "Trade Reform and Environmental Externalities in General Equilibrium: Analysis for an Archetype Poor Tropical Country." *Environment and Development Economics*, *5*, 377-404.

Lucas, Robert E. B., David, Wheeler. & Hemamala, Hettige. (1992). Economic Development, Environmental Regulation, and the International Migration of Toxic Industrial Pollution 1960-1988. *World Development Report No. 1062*, Washington D.C.: World Bank.

Markusen, James R. (1984). "Multinationals, Multiplant Economies and the Gains from Trade." *Journal of International Economics* *16* 205-226.

—. (1981). "Trade and the Gains from Trade with Imperfect Competition." *Journal of International Economics* *11*, 531-551.

Muradian, Roldan. & Joan, Martinez-Alier. (2001). "Trade and the Environment: from a 'Southern' Perspective." *Ecological Economics*, *36* 281-297.

Moon, Wanki. (2011). Is Agriculture Compatible with Free Trade? *Ecological Economics* 71: 13-24.

North, Douglass C. (1994). "Economic Performance through Time." *American Economic Review*, *84*, 359-368.

Rodrik, Dani. (2006). "Goodbye Washington Consensus, Hello Washington Confusion?" *Journal of Economic Literature*, *44*, 973-987.

Ropke, Inge. (1994). "Trade, Development, and Sustainability: A Critical Assessment of the Free Trade Dogma." *Ecological Economics*, *9* 13-22.

Seidl, Irmi. & Clement, Tisdell. (1999). "Carrying Capacity Reconsidered: from Malthus' Population Theory to Cultural Carrying Capacity." *Ecological Economics*, *31*, 395-408.

Seldon, Thomas M. & Daqing, Song. (1995). "Neoclassical Growth, the J Curve for Abatement and the Inverted U Curve for Pollution." *Journal of Environmental Economics and Management* 29 162-168.

Self, Sharmistha. & Richard, Grabowski. (2007). "Economic Development and the Role of Agricultural Technology." *Agricultural Economics*, *36*, 395-404.

Serra, Narcis. & Joseph, E. Stiglitz. (2008). "Introduction: From the Washington Consensus Towards a New Global Governance." In *The Washington Consensus Reconsidered*, eds. Narcis.

Serra & Joseph E. Stiglitz. Oxford, UK: Oxford University Press.

Smulders, Jack., Daan van Soest & C. A. A. M. Withagen. (2004). "International Trade, Species Diversity and Habitat Conservation." *Journal of Environmental Economics and Management*, *48*, 891-910.

Stiglitz, Joseph E. (1998a). "More Instruments and Broader Goals: Moving Toward the Post-Washington Consensus." *The WIDER Annual Lectures*. Helsinki, Finland: World Institute for Development Economics Research.

—. (1998b). "Towards a New paradigm for Development: Strategies, Policies and Processes." *The Raul Prebisch Lectures.* Geneva, Switzerland: UNCTAD.

Stern, David I. (2004). "The Rise and Fall of the Environmental Kuznets Curve." *World Development*, *32* 1419-1439.

—. (1998). "Progress on the Environmental Kuznets Curve?" *Environment and Development Economics*, *3* 173-196.

Stern, David I. & Michael S. Common. (2001). "Is there an Environmental Kuznets Curve for Sulfer?" *Journal of Environmental Economics and Management*, *41* 162-178.

Stern, David I., Michael, S. Common. & Edward, B. Barbier. (1996). "Economic Growth and Environmental Degradation: The Environmental

Kuznets Curve and Sustainable Development." *World Development 24* 1151-1160.

Tisdell, Clement. (2001). "Globalization and Sustainability: Environmental Kuznets Curve and the WTO." *Ecological Economics, 39* 185-196.

Tiffin, Richard. & Xavier, Irz. (2006). "Is Agriculture the Engine of Growth?" *Agricultural Economics, 35*, 79-89.

Wade, Robert. (1996). "Japan, the World Bank and the Art of Paradigm Maintenance: The East Asian Miracle in Political Perspective." *New Left Review*, 3-36.

Williamson, John. (1990). "What Washington Means by Policy Reform." In John Williamson, ed., *Latin American Adjustment: How Much Has Happened?*, eds. John Williamson. Washington, DC. Institute for International Economics.

In: Trade Liberalization
Editor: Pauline Santos
ISBN: 978-1-63483-867-2

Chapter 4

TRADE LIBERALIZATION AND THE STRUCTURE OF MANUFACTURING EXPORTS IN AUSTRALIA

Andrew Marks*
University of Western Sydney, Australia

ABSTRACT

Trade liberalization has been at the epicentre of the restructuring of manufacturing exports from the simply transformed to the elaborately transformed manufacturing products which are more competitive on the international market. This has sharpened the export focus of the Australian manufacturing sector thereby providing a platform for stronger output and employment growth. However, manufacturing products as a proportion of total exports has exhibited a downward trend which has led to the persistence of a narrow primary product export base. This in turn has resulted in sustained terms of trade-induced income losses and fluctuations in export revenue and hence output and employment growth.

* Email: a.marks@uws.edu.au.

1. INTRODUCTION

Numerous studies of the impact of trade liberalization on the Australian manufacturing sector have been undertaken since the progressive reduction in import protection levels began in 1971. They include Swan and Zietch (1992), Bullock, Grenville and Heenan (1993) and Athukorala (1995) among others which reveal the integral role of the move towards free trade in accelerating the manufacturing export growth rate for various sub periods in the eighteen years to 1994. Marks and Sadeghi (1998) complement this result by using a single equation export model to highlight a statistically significant inverse relationship between trade liberalization and export oriented manufacturing production in the period 1980(1)-1996(2), with this relationship becoming more pronounced in the latter part of this period to reflect the impact of the accumulated reductions in import protection levels. In another study, Chand (1999) uses a production function framework to disclose a statistically negative relationship between the nominal rate of assistance and multi-factor productivity (MFP) growth in the manufacturing sector and its 6 two digit Australian Standard Industrial Classification (ASIC) subdivisions in the period 1968/69-1994/95. This result overlaps with the study by Paul and Marks (2009) who use a cost function approach to reveal the pivotal role of trade liberalization in stimulating (MFP) growth and compressing costs in the manufacturing sector and its 7 two digit Australian and New Zealand Industrial Classification (ANZIC) subdivisions in the period 1968/69-2000/01. Moreover, Gaston (1998) emphasizes the employment losses emanating from the move towards free trade by utilizing a single equation model to reveal a statistically significant positive relationship between falling levels of import protection and employment in the manufacturing sector and its 12 two digit (ASIC) subdivisions in the period 1974/75-1991/92. This result is consistent with Jayanthakumaran (2006) who uses a dynamic model of labor demand to highlight the dampening effect of trade liberalization on employment due to more efficient use of labor as mirrored in rising labor productivity.

Chand (1999) and Paul and Marks (2009) complement these studies by explaining the transmission mechanism through which trade liberalization has been promoting the Australian manufacturing sector's export competitiveness. The first study estimates a Cobb Douglass production function both in levels (with constant returns to scale) and growth rates incorporating industry specific fixed effects, to highlight the underlying importance of trade liberalization (using the nominal rate of assistance) in driving higher multifactor productivity (MFP) growth in this sector and its two digit (ANZIC) subdivisions in the period 1968/69-1994/95. A similar result has been reached by (Paul and Marks 2009) who use a cost function approach to assess the impact of openness (using an array of different measures) on cost savings (dual) and MFP output enhancing (primal) effects in the Australian manufacturing sector and its two digit ANZIC subdivisions in the more recent period 1968/69-2000/01. The empirical results reveal a statistically significant positive relationship between the various measures of openness and costs of production and a statistically significant inverse relationship between openness and MFP. The current study seeks to complement the existing studies of the impact of trade liberalization on the Australian manufacturing sector by assessing the impact on the structure of exports of this sector. The rest of the chapter is structured as follows. Section 2 will canvas the theory of international trade and with the following section assessing the impact of trade liberalization on the structure of manufacturing exports. Section 4 will focus on the implications for policy of the main results of the chapter with the final section providing an overview of the important revelations.

2. The Theory of International Trade

International trade theory emphasizes that liberalizing trade will increase import competition thereby leading to the restructuring of production from the economic activities with the least to those with the greatest comparative advantage on the international market. This will be underpinned by specialization in the production of the internationally more competitive products thereby sharpening the export focus of the economy. An analogous situation is expected when a particular sector is exposed to free trade. Thus, liberalizing trade in relation to the Australian manufacturing sector is also expected to lead to the restructuring of production towards the internationally more competitive products thereby raising its export profile.

3. The Impact of Trade Liberalization on the Structure of Manufacturing Exports

This section will examine various dimensions of the impact of trade liberalization on the structure of manufacturing exports. Towards this end, the following figure displays changes in the structure of manufacturing exports in the period 1989/90-2013/14.

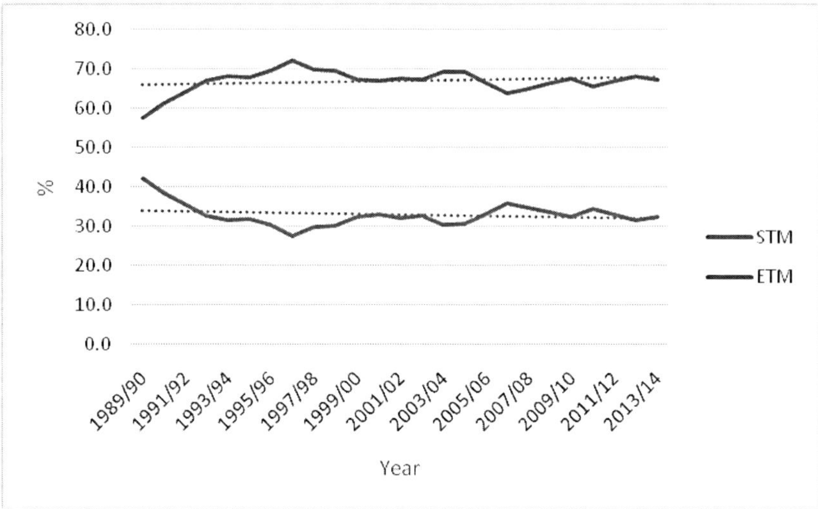

Source:dfat.gov.au.

Figure 1. ETM and STM as a Proportion of Total Manufacturing Exports.

Figure 1 depicts elaborately transformed manufacturing (ETM) exports have steadily increased their contribution whilst simply transformed manufacturing (STM) exports have progressively reduced their contribution to manufacturing exports.[1] This is confirmed by the upward trend in ETM exports and the downward trend in STM exports. This constitutes a positive impact of trade liberalization on the structure of manufacturing export as ETM products are higher value added and hence internationally more competitive compared to the STM products. As a result, the former category has exhibited a superior (real) export growth rate of 7.1 percent compared to the lower 3.2 percent export growth rate of STM exports.

The improvement in the structure of manufacturing exports in favor of ETMs highlights the instrumental role of trade liberalization in prompting firms to re-allocate resources from the least competitive STMs which are more susceptible to the stronger import competition to the production and export of

[1]ETM exports are defined as the 3 digit subdivisions of mineral manufactures, chemicals and other semi manufactures, engineering products (excluding household equipment) and other. STM exports are defined as the 3 digit subdivisions of mineral manufactures and metals, chemicals and other semi manufactures and other.

the internationally more competitive ETM products. Nevertheless, it is important to emphasize that industry policy initiatives such as tax incentives for investment and research and development expenditure and export subsidies have cushioned the impact of the stronger import competition thereby providing the opportunity for the manufacturing sector to effectively respond by promoting ETM exports. Indeed, Sheehan, Pappas and Cheng (1994) attribute a major role to this policy in accelerating the ETM export growth rate in the period 1985-93. The persistence with industry policy beyond this period is likely to underscore its importance in contributing to the impressive 7.1 percent growth rate in these types of exports in the more recent period of 1989/90-2013/14.

Various microeconomic reform measures have combined with trade liberalization and the reinforcing industry policy initiatives to bolster the export competitiveness of ETMs. They include the deregulation of markets such as infrastructure services, improved labor market flexibility, education and training reforms to raise the skill level of the labor force, privatization and greater commercial pressure on government business enterprises to improve economic efficiency. For example, improved labor market flexibility has led to progressive move from a centralized to decentralized industrial relations system where negotiations for higher wages and improved working conditions between trade unions and employees has increasingly occurred at the enterprise level. The objective has been to link wage increases and improvements in working conditions to productivity offsets in order neutralize the higher labor costs on total costs and thereby preserve international competitiveness. Moreover, Forsyth (2000) notes the deregulation of infrastructure services such as transportation, storage, telecommunications and energy has led to higher productivity in various sub periods from the mid-1980s to the late 1990s, a trend which is likely to have continued in light of the maintenance of a highly competitive environment. This combats the costs of using these infrastructure services as inputs into the production process throughout the economy which includes firms engaged in exporting ETMs thereby augmenting their international competitiveness. Finally, the higher export profile of ETM products has been facilitated by the generally buoyant international economic conditions prevailing and the prevalence of free trade in manufacturing products which was completed during the Tokyo round of trade negotiations in 1979 under the auspicious of the General Agreement on Tariffs and Trade (G.A.T.T). It should be noted these two external developments constitute critical complements to domestic policy in improving the export performance of ETMs.

It is interesting to note the rising proportion of ETM to manufacturing exports conceals the varied contribution of its four three digit Standard International Trade Classification (SITC) subdivisions. This is highlighted by the following figure.[2]

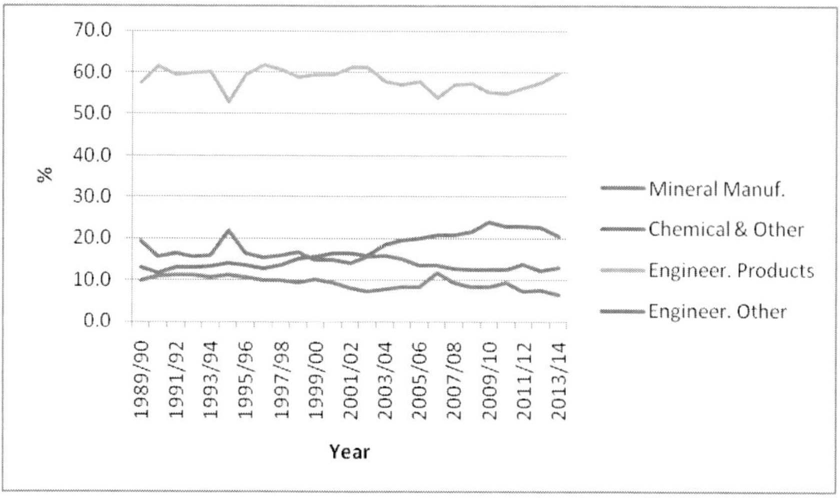

Source:dfat.gov.au.

Figure 2. Mineral Manufacturing, Chemical and Other, Engineering and Other Subdivisions as a Proportion of ETM Exports.

The interesting trends of figure 2 include the limited change in the subdivisions engineering products and mineral manufacturing whilst the chemical and other subdivision has progressively increased its contribution to ETM exports. Finally, the other subdivision has steadily reduced its contribution.

The restructuring of manufacturing exports towards the internationally more competitive ETMs is likely to have sharpened the export focus of the manufacturing sector. This is depicted in the period 1989/90-2013/14 by figure 3.

[2] These subdivisions are defined as Standard International Trade Classification (SITC) 241 mineral manufactures, SITC 242 chemicals and other semi manufactures, SITC 243 engineering products (excluding household equipment) and SITC 244 other.

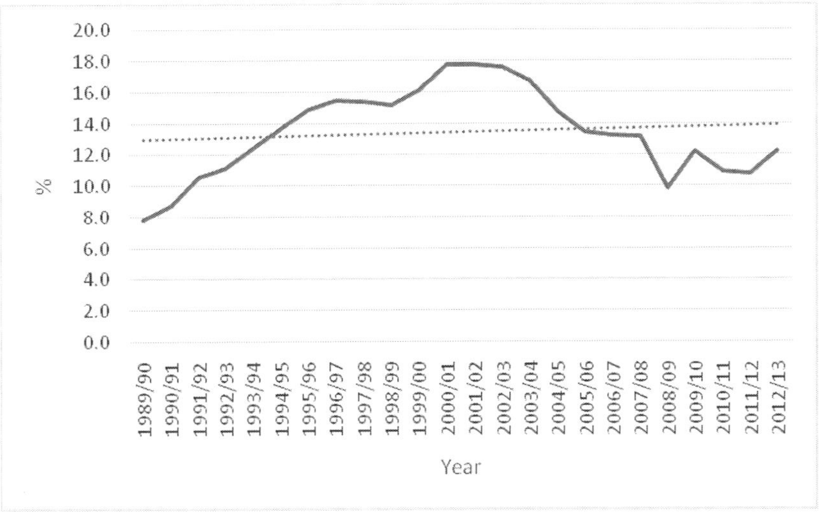

Source: deft.gov.au.

Figure 3. Export Oriented Manufacturing Production.

Figure 3 depicts a marginal improvement in export oriented manufacturing production.[3] Of interest is the appreciable rise in the period 1989/90-2000/01 which appears to fundamentally be explained by the strong growth in ETM exports from a low base. Specifically, the (real) growth rate in this category of manufacturing exports has been 12.8 percent compared to 4.2 percent for STMs. This strong export performance of ETMs and STMs has been facilitated by the buoyant international economic conditions prevailing and the relatively low value of the exchange rate which preserves export competitiveness. However, the relatively stronger export growth rate of ETMs appears to mirror the higher value added of these products which are characterized by higher income elasticity of demand on the international market compared to STMs. The third interesting feature of figure 3 is the downturn in export oriented production since 2000/01 which appears to basically rcflcct the resource boom-induced large appreciation of the Australian dollar that has had a significant dampening effect on manufacturing

[3] Export oriented manufacturing production is calculated as real manufacturing exports as a proportion of real turnover. Manufacturing export are defined as the nominal value of the ETM and STM exports. The real value of manufacturing exports has been derived by deflating the nominal value by the non-rural export price deflator in 1989/90 prices. Real turnover has been calculated as the nominal value deflated by the GDP deflator in 1989/90 prices.

exports. This effect has been compounded by the strong growth in domestic demand which tends to discourage exports.

Nevertheless, the higher export profile of the Australian manufacturing sector has a number of positive effects. First, the increased penetration of the international market leads to stronger output and employment growth as this sector's orientation has been skewed more so towards the larger international market. Furthermore, the higher export profile has been underpinned by the restructuring of production from STMs to ETMs which implies a higher degree of specialization in production that leads to the cost benefits of large scale production thereby reinforcing export competitiveness. The importance of this factor is highlighted by Caves (1984) who discloses the relatively small scale of production and hence higher than otherwise costs prevailing in the Australian manufacturing sector which acts as a major barrier to export growth. Furthermore, the sharper export focus implies quicker growth in manufacturing production which in turn provides a major stimulus to domestic economic activity due to the external linkages with other segments of the economy. This is highlighted by the input/output analysis of the Australian Bureau of Statistics (ABS) ABS (2009/10) which reveals that manufacturing output required $55.40 of intermediate goods from other sectors in 2009/10. In particular, this consists of $6.60 from the agriculture sector, $7.90 from the mining sector and $21.50 from the services sector whilst $19.50 of manufacturing output was used as intermediate goods by other sectors. Of note is the particularly strong linkage effect with the services sector. This result is consistent with (Cohen and Zysman 1987) who emphasize the important stimulatory impact of manufacturing activity on the services sector in other western market economies. Thus, higher manufacturing exports and hence production will provide a particularly strong stimulus to output and employment growth in the Australian economy via its linkage to various sectors of the economy.

It is important to emphasize the inroads made by ETM exports in the international market is likely to provide a sufficiently strong incentive for firms to continue to combat costs and improve the quality of output in order to preserve and expand their export gains. Of overriding importance however is that this will provide a platform for quicker and sustainable output and employment growth due to the stronger reliance on the large international market. Nevertheless, one offsetting cost of the sharper export focus of the Australian manufacturing sector is the greater vulnerability to changes in international economic conditions. For example, a deep international recession will lead to a downturn in domestic output and employment growth with this effect more pronounced due to the increasing reliance of manufacturing production on the world economy and the extensive linkage effects with other sectors of the economy.

Finally, it is important to emphasize the positive impact of trade liberalization in restructuring manufacturing exports from STMs to the internationally more competitive ETM products has sharpened the export focus of the Australian manufacturing sector. These revelations in turn makes them consistent with the theory of international trade as espoused in section 2.

However, the rising export orientation of the Australian manufacturing sector has not been sufficiently strong to improve the structure of exports. This is depicted in the period 1989/90-2013/14 by the following figure.

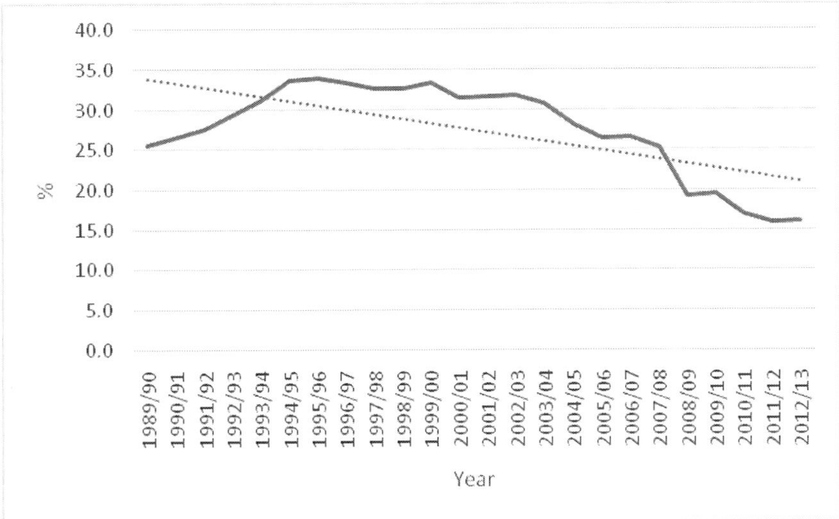

Source: dfat.gov.au.

Figure 4. Manufacturing as a Proportion of Total Exports.

There are a number of dimensions related to figure 4 which are interesting to note. They include the higher contribution of manufacturing to total exports in the period 1989/90-1994/95 and the subsequent decline. The former dimension is largely explained by the acceleration in the ETM export growth rate which has exceeded that of total exports. The latter dimension reflects the decline in the contribution of manufacturing to total exports which has been more pronounced since 2002/03 and appears to fundamentally reflect the large appreciation of the exchange rate due to the commodity price boom (i.e., the Australian currency is sensitive to commodity price changes) and domestic demand buoyancy. The former factor leads to the deterioration in export competitiveness which appears to have had a particularly strong dampening effect on manufacturing exports whilst the latter factor compounds this problem by encouraging firms to focus on the domestic rather than international market. Finally, of crucial importance is that the declining trend in the proportion of exports attributable to manufacturing products conceals the interesting phenomenon whereby manufacturing exports have been growing although at a relatively slower rate than overall exports.

4. Implications for Policy of the Main Results

The current structure of exports therefore implies the export base is dominated by primary products whose price however increases relatively slower than manufacturing products on the international market thereby leading to forgone export revenue and hence output and employment gains. This problem has been exposed by Hamilton (1991), Hart (1993) and Hart and Marks (1999) who advocate the need to implement industry policy initiatives to accelerate manufacturing export growth and hence broaden the export base in order to alleviate the deterioration in the terms of trade-induced income losses. The dominance of primary exports also subjects Australia to the greater variability in primary product prices on the international market which in turn leads to fluctuations in export revenue and hence output and employment growth. This problem has been confirmed in the Australian context by Hart (1993) and Hanpson (2012). Finally, the low contribution of manufacturing to total exports implies the existence of unrealized potential to significantly increase manufacturing exports which will lead to appreciable output and employment growth. This is more so the case due to the extensive linkage effects of manufacturing production with other sectors of the economy.

There is a need therefore to implement policies to stimulate manufacturing and in particular the ETM export growth rate to arrest and eventually eliminate these problems. This challenge can be effectively confronted by implementing a vigorous policy response which includes industry policy initiatives as part of an overall strategy to bolster ETM export growth. These initiatives include tax, subsidies and other incentives to influence the allocation of resources towards manufacturing exports. The effectiveness of industry policy in stimulating manufacturing exports is highlighted by the experience of a number of countries. For example, Jomo (2001) highlights the positive impact of industry policy initiatives in stimulating manufacturing exports and hence economic growth in the in the high performing Asian economies (HPAEs) of S. Korea and Taiwan, Japan, Hong Kong, Singapore, Malaysia, Thailand and Indonesia in the period 1965-1990. Specifically, incentives were provided such as the initial restriction of foreign direct investment (FDI) and temporary import protection measures in order to encourage the growth of domestic firms which in turn would provide them with a competitive advantage on the international market via the scale factor which minimizes costs. Furthermore, direct incentives for exports such as tariff exemption for imports of capital and intermediate goods and exchange rate depreciation were also provided to reinforce export competitiveness. Restrictions on FDI were subsequently relaxed with inflows to be specifically export focused in export processing zones (EPZs) in order to provide further imputes to export growth. Towards this end, various incentives were provided such as tax holidays and tariff exemptions for imported capital and intermediate goods. An important dimension of this strategy was the use of industry policy to progressively move up the value added chain in order to continuously improve international competitiveness. In another study, Weiss and Jahilian (2004) emphasize the importance of industry policy in explaining East and South East Asia's superior economic growth performance relative to Latin American countries in the period of the early 1980s to late 1990s. Moreover, Hampson (2012) highlights the effectiveness of this policy in promoting manufacturing exports in both the HPAEs and Scandinavian countries. International experience therefore indicates the need for Australia to consider implementing industry policy as part of an overall strategy to accelerate the manufacturing export growth rate and thereby maximize and stabilize export revenue and hence output and employment growth. The persistent failure of the market to achieve this critical outcome renders this strategy all the more relevant.

5. Overview of Main Results

Trade liberalization has played a pivotal role in prompting an improvement in the structure of manufacturing exports towards the internationally more competitive ETMs. This has led to the acceleration in the export growth rate of these products thereby underpinning the sharper export focus of the Australian manufacturing sector. However, the growth in manufacturing exports has not been sufficiently strong to improve the structure of exports thereby leading to the persistence of a narrow primary product dominated export base. This has subjected Australia to slower export revenue and hence output and employment growth due to the relatively slower increase in primary compared to manufacturing product prices on the international market. Furthermore, the gyrations in primary product prices on the international market have led to fluctuations in export revenue and hence output and employment growth. These two serious problems therefore necessitate a vigorous policy response in order to alleviate and eventually eliminate their impact on the Australian economy. This includes implementing industry policy as part of a package of measures to stimulate manufacturing and in particular the ETM export growth rate.

REFERENCES

Australian Bureau of Statistics 2009/10, Australian National Accounts, Input, Output Tables Cat. No. 5204.0, and 5.001, Canberra.

Athokurala, P. 1995, 'Internationalisation and Structural Adoption,' *Economic Papers* vol.14. pp.1-11.

Bullock, M., Grenville, S. and Heenan, G. 1993, 'The Exchange Rate and the Current Account,' in *The Exchange Rate, International Trade and the Balance of Payments*, Reserve Bank of Australia, Sydney, ed. A. Blundell-Wignal.

Caves, R.E. 1984, 'Scale, openness and productivity in manufacturing industries in the Australian economy,' in A View From the North (eds.) R.E. Caves and L.B. Krause, Allen and Unwin, Sydney, pp. 313-348.

Chand, S. 1999, 'Trade Liberalisation and Productivity Growth: Time Series Evidence from Australia,' *Economic Record*, vol. 75, pp.129-48.

Cohen, S.S. and Zysman, J. 1987, Manufacturing Matters – The Myth of the Post-Industrial Economy,' Basic Books Inc, New York. www.dfat.au - Department of Foreign Affairs and Trade.

Forsyth, P. 2000, 'Microeconomic Policies and Structural Reform,' Gruen, D and Shrestha, S. (eds.), The Australian Economy in the 1990s, RBA, Sydney

Hamilton, C. 1991, 'Strategic trade policy and its relevance in Australia' in C. Hamilton (ed.), The Economic Dynamics of Australian Industry, Allen and Unwin, Sydney, pp.

Hampson, I. 2012, ' Industry policy under economic liberalism: policy development in the Prime Minister's manufacturing task force,' *Economic and Labour Relations Review* 23: 39-56.

Hart, N. 1993, 'Australia's current account difficulties and the role of trade and industry policy,' *Economic Papers* 12: 32-46.

Hart, N. and Marks, A. 1999,' Australia's current account deficit, national savings and industry policy,' *The Economic and Labour Relations Review* 10:278-295.

Jomo, K.S. 2001, 'Rethinking the role of government policy in southeast Asia' in Stiglitz J.E. and Yusuf S. (eds), Rethinking the east Asian miracle, Oxford University Press, New York and World Bank, Washington DC, pp 461-508.

Marks, A., and Sadeghi M. 1998, 'Testing the Olson Hypothesis within the Australian Context,' *Australian Economic Review*, vol.31, pp.130-44.

Paul,S., and Marks, A. 2009, 'Modeling Productivity Effects of Trade Openness: A Dual Approach,' *Australian Economic Papers*, vol.48, pp.105-123.

Sheehan, P.J., Pappas N. and Cheng E. 1994, The Rebirth of Australian Industry, Centre for Strategic Economic Studies, Melbourne.

Weiss, J. and Jalilian, H. 2004, 'Industrialization in an age of Globalization: Some comparisons between East and South East Asia and Latin America,' *Oxford Development Studies*, 32:283-307.

Swan, P. and Zeitch J. 1992, 'The Emerging Australian Manufacturing Export Response to Microeconomic Reform,' *Australian Journal of Management*, vol.17, pp.21-41.

BIBLIOGRAPHY

15 Years of the Information Technology Agreement: trade, innovation and global production networks. LCCN: 2012449456 Main title: 15 Years of the Information Technology Agreement: trade, innovation and global production networks. Published/Created: Geneva: World Trade Organization, c2012. Description: 108 p.: col. ill.; 30 cm. Links: http://wto.org/english/res_e/publications_e/ita15years_2012_e.htm Connect to online version. ISBN: 9789287038265 (pbk.) 9287038260 (pbk.) LC classification: K4611.I54 A15 2012 Other title: Fifteen years of the Information Technology Agreement Related names: World Trade Organization. Summary: "The Information and Technology Agreement (ITA) was finalized at the first WTO Ministerial Conference, in Singapore, in 1996, committing its participants to completely eliminate duties on certain information technology products. In its 15 years, the ITA has promoted affordable access to a wide range of technologies, encouraging closer cooperation between developed and developing countries. As production networks become increasingly global, the ITA will continue to facilitate the shift from products made in a specific country to "made in the world." To mark the 15th anniversary of the ITA, this publication charts the political and technical obstacles which were overcome during the creation of the Agreement and the issues which still need to be resolved. It details the establishment of the ITA Committee and how the Agreement is implemented, and investigates the impact the ITA

has had on trade liberalization and innovation. The publication also examines the effect information technology has had on global production networks and what this means for developing countries and the ITA."--Back cover. Contents: The road to the Information Technology Agreement -- The ITA committee: 15 years of encouraging trade -- The impact of the trade liberalization brought by the ITA -- The ITA and innovation -- Global production networks, electronic products and developing countries Subjects: Information Technology Agreement (1996) Tariff on information technology products. Notes: Title from cover. Includes bibliographical references.

Applied trade policy modeling in 16 countries: insights and impacts from World Bank CGE based projects LCCN: 2013047862 Personal name: Tarr, David G. Main title: Applied trade policy modeling in 16 countries: insights and impacts from World Bank CGE based projects/David G. Tarr; consultant and former lead economist, The World Bank, USA. Published/Produced: New Jersey; London; Singapore; Beijing; Shanghai; Hong Kong; Taipei; Chennai: World Scientific, [2014] ©2014 Description: vii, 539 pages: illustrations; 25 cm. ISBN: 9789814551427 (hbk.) 9814551422 (hbk.) LC classification: HF1411 .T288 2014 Other title: Applied trade policy modeling in sixteen countries Contents: Welfare costs of US quotas in textiles, steel and auto/J. Melo and D. G. Tarr -- Reforming Hungarian agricultural trade policy: a quantitative evaluation/M. Morkre and D. G. Tarr -- Second-best foreign exchange policy in the presence of domestic price controls and export subsidies/ D. G. Tarr -- Trade reform in the partially liberalized economy of Turkey/G. W. Harrison, T. F. Rutherford and D. G. Tarr -- The impact of liberalizing barriers to foreign direct investment in services: the case of Russian accession to the World Trade Organization/J. Jensen, T. F. Rutherford and D. G. Tarr -- Regional impacts of liberalization of barriers against foreign direct investment in services: the case of Russia's accession to the WTO/T. R. Rutherford and D. G. Tarr -- Impact of local content restrictions and barriers against foreign direct investment in services: the case of Kazakhstan accession to the WTO/J. Jensen and D. G. Tarr -- Modeling services liberalization: the case of Tanzania/J. Jensen, T. F. Rutherford and D. G. Tarr -- Trade policy and poverty reduction in Brazil/G. W. Harrison, T. F. Rutherford, D. G. Tarr and A. Gurgel -- Trade liberalization, poverty and efficient equity/G. W. Harrison, T. F. Rutherford and D. G. Tarr -- Poverty effects of Russia's WTO accession: modeling real households with endogenous productivity effects/T. F. Rutherford and D. G. Tarr -- Trade, exchange rate and energy pricing reform in Iran: potentially large efficiency effects and gains to the poor/J. Jensen and D. G. Tarr -- Trade policy options for Chile: the importance of market access/G. W. Harrison, T. F. Rutherford and D. G. Tarr -- Increased competition and completion of the market in the European Union: static and steady state effects/G. W. Harrison, T. F. Rutherford and D. G. Tarr -- Economic implications for Turkey of a customs union with the European Union/G. W. Harrison, T. F. Rutherford and D. G. Tarr -- Morocco's free trade agreement with the EU: a quantitative assessment/T. F. Rutherford, E. Elizabet Rutstrom and D. G. Tarr -- Introduction and tables to services liberalization in preferential trade agreements: the case of Kenya/E. J. Balistreri and D. G. Tarr -- Deep trade policy options for Armenia: the importance of trade facilitation, services and standards liberalization/J. Jensen and D. G. Tarr -- The Eurasian customs union among Russia, Belarus and Kazakhstan: can it succeed where its predecessor failed?/D. G. Tarr. Subjects: Commercial policy. International trade--Econometric models. Computable general equilibrium models. Notes: Includes bibliographical pages and index. Series: World Scientific studies in international economics 1793-3641; vol. 34

Building legislative coalitions for free trade in Asia: globalization as legislation LCCN: 2015003325 Personal name: Naoi, Megumi 1973- Main title: Building legislative coalitions for free trade in Asia: globalization as legislation/Megumi Naoi. Published/Produced: New York, NY: Cambridge University Press 2015. Description: pages cm Links: Cover image http://assets.cambridge.org/97811070/37038/cover/9781107037038.jpg ISBN: 9781107037038 (hardback) LC classification: JQ1669.P53 N36 2015 Summary: "What accounts for the large reduction in trade barriers among new democracies in Asia after World War II? Using new data from Japan and Thailand, this book provides a surprising answer: politicians, especially party leaders, liberalized trade by buying off legislative support with side-payments such as pork barrel projects. Trade liberalization was a legislative triumph, not an executive achievement. This finding challenges the conventional "insulation" argument, which posits that insulating executives from special interest groups and voters is the key to successful trade liberalization. By contrast, this book demonstrates that party leaders built open economy coalitions with legislators by feeding legislators' rent-seeking desires with side-payments rather than depriving their appetites. This book unravels the political foundations of open economy"--Provided by publisher. Contents: Machine generated contents note: Part I. Building Open Economy Coalitions: 1. Optimal use of pork, policy, and institutional reforms; Part II. Empirical Evidence: 2. Use of pork as side-payment; 3. Pro-loser policy during hard times; 4. Helping losers survive elections: use of institutional reforms; 5. Japanese legislators in rival regions; 6. Thai legislators' position-taking on foreign retail investment; Part III. Discussion: 7. Globalization as legislation: discussion. Subjects: Political planning--Japan. Political planning--Thailand. Political leadership--Japan. Political leadership--Thailand. Free trade--Political aspects--Japan. Free trade--Political aspects--Thailand. Finance, Public--Japan. Finance, Public--Thailand. Political Science/Economic Conditions. Japan--Appropriations and expenditures. Thailand--Appropriations and expenditures. Notes: Includes bibliographical references and index.

Economic and trade policies in the Arab world: employment, poverty reduction and integration LCCN: 2011043591 Main title: Economic and trade policies in the Arab world: employment, poverty reduction and integration/[edited by] Mahmoud A.T. Elkhafif, Sahar Taghdisi Rad and Mutasim Elagraa. Edition: 1st ed. Published/Created: New York: Routledge 2012. Description: xix, 348 p.: ill.; 24 cm. ISBN: 9780415519458 (hbk) 9780203120927 (ebk) LC classification: HC498 .E22 2012 Related names: Elkhafif, Mahmoud A. T. Taghdisi-Rad, Sahar. Elagraa, Mutasim 1963-

Contents: Introduction: promoting sub-regional growth-oriented economic and trade policies towards achieving the Millennium Development Goals in selected Arab countries/by Hanaa Kheir-El-Din and Fadle Naqib -- Investigating the relationship between trade and poverty: the case of Egypt -- Employment and poverty effects of trade and investment policies in Jordan -- Process and implications of Morocco's economic and trade liberalization -- Economic and trade policy-making under occupation in the Palestinian Territory -- Trade policy, regional integration and pro-poor growth: an empirical analysis for Sudan 1970-2007 -- Quantitative study: Arab trade: data, models and issues -- Conclusion: development strategy for poverty reduction and Arab integration/by Hanaa Kheir El-Din and Fadle Naqib. Subjects: Foreign trade and employment--Arab countries. Poverty--Arab countries. Arab countries--Economic policy. Notes: Includes bibliographical references and index. Series: The Routledge political economy of the Middle East and North Africa series; 11 Routledge political economy of the Middle East and North Africa series; 11.

Economic management in Pakistan: general economic management, industrial revival, MFN & trade liberalization with India LCCN: 2014311067 Personal name: Mannoo, Kamal, author. Main title: Economic management in Pakistan: general economic management, industrial revival, MFN & trade liberalization with India/Dr. Kamal Mannoo. Edition: First edition. Published/Produced: Lahore: Bookland 2013. Description: xiv 178 pages; 23 cm ISBN: 9789695381021 9695381022 LC classification: HC440.5 .M32 2013 Subjects: Economic policy. Industrial policy--Pakistan. Favored nation clause--India. Pakistan--Economic policy. Notes: Includes bibliographical references (pages 175-178).

Essentials of exporting and importing: U.S. trade policies, procedures, and practices LCCN: 2014010909 Personal name: Shoemack, Harvey R. Main title: Essentials of exporting and importing: U.S. trade policies, procedures, and practices/Harvey Shoemack, Patricia Mink Rath. Edition: Second edition. Published/Produced: New York: Fairchild Books 2014. Description: xvi, 331 pages: illustrations; 23 cm ISBN: 9781609018894 (paperback) LC classification: HF1416.5 .S56 2014 Related names: Rath, Patricia Mink. Summary: "International business, especially the export-import trade, is no longer an option, but a necessity for today's apparel industry to grow and generate profits or just to survive in the global marketplace. The decision to export or import is best based on a company or individual entrepreneur's careful and thorough analysis of its internal and external resources and capabilities. Essentials of Exporting and Importing provides the merchandising, marketing, or business student a practical, basic guide for importing and exporting products, services, or technology in a global economy"-- Provided by publisher. Contents: Machine generated contents note: -- Introduction Preface Acknowledgments Part I: Globalization and World Trade Chapter 1: An Overview of Global Business Today Chapter 2: Globalization and World Trade Liberalization Chapter 3: The U.S. Role in Global Trade Part II: U.S. Exporting Policies and Procedures Chapter 4: Basics of Exporting Chapter 5: U.S. Export Controls and Procedures Part III: Importing into the United States Chapter 6: Basics of Importing into the United States Chapter 7: Entering the Import Business Chapter 8: Navigating the Maze of Import Controls Part IV: Trade Finance Chapter 9: Getting Paid or Paying for Exports or Imports Chapter 10: Case Studies Glossary Credits Index. Subjects: Exports--United States. Imports--United States. Foreign trade regulation--United States. Business & Economics/Industries/Fashion & Textile Industry. Business & Economics/General. United States--Commerce. Notes: Includes index.

Globalization, trade, and poverty in Ghana LCCN: 2012312400 Main title: Globalization, trade, and poverty in Ghana/edited by Charles Ackah and Ernest Aryeetey. Published/Created: Ottawa: International Development Research Centre; Accra, Ghana: Sub-Saharan Publishers 2012. Description: vi 250 p.: ill.; 25 cm. Links: Table of contents only http://www.loc.gov/catdir/toc/fy13pdf06/2012312400.html ISBN: 9789988647360 9988647360 LC classification: HC1060 .G56 2012 Related names: Ackah, Charles. Aryeetey, Ernest 1955- Contents: Introduction and overview/Charles Ackah and Ernest Aryeetey -- An overview of trade policies and developments in Ghana/Albert Laryea and Sarah Akuoni -- Trends in growth, employment and poverty in Ghana/Charles Ackah and William Baah-Boateng -- Wage and employment effects of trade liberalization: the case of Ghanaian manufacturing/Charles Ackah, Ernest Aryeetey and Kwadwo Opoku -- The effects of trade liberalization on the return to education in Ghana/Charles Ackah, Oliver Morrissey and Simon Appleton -- Trade, trade policy and total factor productivity: the case of Ghanaian manufacturing firms/Charles Ackah, Ernest Aryeetey and Oliver Morrissey -- The impact of the elimination of trade taxes on poverty and income distribution in Ghana/Vijay Bhasin -- Food prices, tax reforms and consumer welfare in Ghana during the 1990s/Charles Ackah and Simon Appleton -- The effect of import liberalization on import tariff yield in Ghana/William Gabriel Brafu-Insaidoo and Camara Kwasi Obeng -- Cash cropping, gender and household welfare: evidence from Ghana/Charles Ackah and Ernest Aryeetey -- The transmission of world commodity prices to domestic markets: household welfare effects in Ghana/Charles Ackah ... [et al.]. Subjects: Poverty--Ghana. Globalization--Social aspects--Ghana. Globalization--Economic aspects--Ghana. Ghana--Commerce. Ghana--Economic conditions. Ghana--Economic policy. Notes: Includes bibliographical references and index.

How to manage an aid exit strategy: the future of development aid LCCN: 2011279817 Personal name: Fee, Derek 1947- Main title: How to manage an aid exit strategy: the future of development aid/Derek Fee. Published/Created: London; New York: Zed Books, c2012. Description: xii 256 p.: ill.; 22 cm. Links: Table of contents only http://www.loc.gov/catdir/enhancements/fy1412/2011279817-t.html Publisher description http://www.loc.gov/catdir/enhancements/fy1412/2011279817-d.html Contributor biographical information http://www.loc.gov/catdir/enhancements/fy1412/2011279817-b.html ISBN: 1780320299 9781780320298 (pbk) 9781780320304 (hbk) 1780320302 LC classification: HC59.7 .F354 2012 Summary: “After almost forty years of development aid most commentators agree that aid as we know it has not worked. Aid fatigue is suffered on both the donor and recipient sides, with a wide divergence between those who call for a radical overhaul of aid delivery methods, those who advocate a complete end to development aid and those who continually demand significant increases in aid flows. How to Manage an Aid Exit Strategy provides a refreshing, insightful and comprehensive analysis of how an exit may actually be possible - drawing on real experience and as such supplying a simple summary of recommended policy steps. The author thoroughly reviews aid for trade, regional integration and microfinance and a host of other solutions that have been proposed - arguing that an exit strategy for both donors and the least developed countries will have to consider the optimal combination of these specific initiatives to best satisfy the necessity of development and at the same time solve the problems of conventional aid."--Publisher's website. Contents: The state of aid -- A short history of development aid -- The development aid business -- Domestic resource mobilization -- Trade liberalization -- The BRICS -- Regional integration -- Microfinance -- Remittances -- Non-governmental organizations and philanthropic foundations -- Towards an aid exit strategy. Subjects: Economic assistance--Developing countries. Economic development--Developing countries. Economic assistance--Developing countries--History. Economic development--Developing countries--Finance--History. Notes: Includes bibliographical references (p. [234]-246) and index.

Impact of trade liberalization on human resource development in the SAARC region. LCCN: 2014311420 Main title: Impact of trade liberalization on human resource development in the SAARC region. Published/Produced: Islamabad: SAARC Human Resource Development Centre, [2013] Description: viii 172 pages; 28 cm LC classification: HD5710.75.P18 I66 2013 Related names: SAARC Human Resource Development Centre. Subjects: Foreign trade and employment--South Asia. Labor market--South Asia. Free trade--South Asia. Notes: Includes bibliographical references (pages 152-155).

International trade negotiations and domestic politics: the intermestic politics of trade liberalization LCCN: 2013004275 Main title:

International trade negotiations and domestic politics: the intermestic politics of trade liberalization/edited by Oluf Langhelle. Published/Produced: New York: Routledge 2014. Description: xviii 240 pages: illustrations; 24 cm. ISBN: 9780415811569 (hardback) LC classification: HF1713 .I568 2014 Related names: Langhelle, Oluf 1964- Contents: Towards the intermestic politics of trade: institutions, ideas, interests and actors/Oluf Langhelle, Hilmar Rommetvedt and Arild Aurvåg Farsund -- The global trade agenda/Oluf Langhelle, Hilmar Rommetvedt and Arild Aurvåg Farsund -- Multilevel negotiations in American trade policy: free trade agreements from Bush to Obama/David M. Olson -- The European Union: balancing trade liberalization and protectionism/Carsten Daugbjerg -- India's trade politics: continuity and change/Amrita Narlikar -- China: an open, confident and booming trading nation/Ning Jun, Yao Lei and Wang Gefei -- Norway: agricultural exceptionalism and the quest for free trade/Arild Aurvåg Farsund -- The intermestic politics of trade/Oluf Langhelle, Arild Aurvåg Farsund and Hilmar Rommetvedt. Subjects: Free trade. International economic relations. Notes: Includes bibliographical references (pages 218-235) and index. Series: Routledge studies in the modern world economy

Liberalization of trade in legal services LCCN: 2013362044 Personal name: Muller, Gilles, author. Main title: Liberalization of trade in legal services/Gilles Muller. Published/Produced: Alphen aan den Rijn, The Netherlands: Wolters Kluwer, Law & Business, [2013] Description: xvii, 313 pages; 25 cm. ISBN: 9789041148537 (hbk.: alk. paper) 9041148531 (hbk.: alk. paper) LC classification: K120 .M85 2013 Contents: Introduction -- Regulation and trade liberalization in legal services -- The GATs and legal services -- The liberalization of legal services under the EU and Swiss (EFTA) preferential trade agreements -- Conclusion. Subjects: Practice of law. Legal services. Foreign trade regulation. International trade. Notes: Includes bibliographical references (pages 267-293). Series: Global trade law series; volume 44 Global trade law series; v. 44.

Linking global trade and human rights: new policy space in hard economic times LCCN: 2013032182 Main title: Linking global trade and human rights: new policy space in hard economic times/Daniel Drache, Centre for Public Policy and Law, York University; Lesley A. Jacobs, Department of Political Science, York University. Published/Produced: New York: Cambridge University Press 2013. Projected pub date: 1311 Description: pages cm ISBN: 9781107047174 (hardback) LC classification: K3943.A6 L56 2013 Related names: Drache, Daniel 1941- editor of compilation. Jacobs, Lesley A., editor of compilation. Summary: "The concept of policy space is critical to understanding the impact of globalization on public policy in the twenty-first century. For the purposes of this book, a policy space is an arena where national governments have the freedom and capacity to design and implement public policies of their own choosing (Grindle & Thomas 1991; Koivusalo et al. 2010). In market economies, policy spaces reflect the insight that certain realms of public life should be governed by collective decision making designed to advance the public interest whereas in other realms markets reign (Drache 2001). The spatial metaphor expresses, in other words, the claim that there are certain sites where government action has legitimacy. Ultimately, national policy spaces matter because they provide opportunities for governments to be innovative in the development of public policy on these sites, especially in terms of advancing social justice goals (Jacobs 2004). The unifying theme of this book is that there are major reconfigurations of social and economic policy spaces for national governments on the international landscape during the hard economic times that follow global financial crises. After the 2008 financial crisis, state action extended into new areas and was being deployed in new and innovative ways from the Cash for Clunkers program in the US to successful anti-poverty programs in Brazil. In India the national Rural Employment Scheme to guarantee a minimum number of paid hours annually to hundreds of millions of its poorest is the largest social welfare scheme in the world"-- Provided by publisher. Contents: Introduction/Daniel Drache and Lesley Jacobs -- Humanising global economic governance/Sol Picciotto -- The promise of linking human rights and trade/Ernest-Ulrich Petersmann -- Free trade agreements and global policy space after the great recession/Jorge Heine and Joseph Turcott -- From Seattle to Occupy: the shifting focus of social protest/Tomer Broude -- What's next for global labour?: power dynamics and industrial relations systems in a hyperglobalized world/Daniel Drache -- Global tobacco control and trade liberalization: new policy spaces?/Lesley Jacobs -- Business, policy spaces, and governance in India/Kuldeep Mathur -- India's pharmaceutical industry: policy space that fosters technological capability/Amit Ray and Saradindu Bhaduri -- Reducing poverty in Brazil: finding policy space for meeting developmental needs/Kathryn Hochstetler -- The global health policy agenda and shrinking policy spaces in the post crisis landscape/Ron Labonté -- The World Trade Organization and food security after the global food crises/Matias Margulis -- Decent work for domestic workers as a new policy space/Adelle Blackett -- Is there policy space for human rights linkages in China's trade and investment strategy?/Ljiljana Biukovic -- Human rights and social justice in China/Pitman Potter -- New policy space for collective bargaining in China/Sarah Biddulph -- Industrial relations in post-transition China: the challenges of inequality and social conflict/Chang-Hee Lee. Subjects: Foreign trade regulation--Congresses. Human rights--Congresses. Law and economic development--Congresses. Law and globalization--Congresses. LAW/International. Notes: "This book has its origins in a major international workshop held at York University in Toronto in October 2011." -- Acknowledgements. Includes bibliographical references and index.

Prelinimary analysis of Pakistan India trade and a viable roadmap for trade liberalization. LCCN: 2014363570 Main title: Prelinimary analysis of Pakistan India trade and a viable roadmap for trade liberalization. Published/Produced: Karachi: Pakistan Business Council, [2014] Description: 102 pages; 30 cm ISBN: 978969 LC classification: HF3790.5.Z7A-.Z7Z (India)+ Related names: Pakistan Business Council. Subjects: Pakistan--Commerce. India--Commerce. Pakistan--Foreign economic relations--India. India--Foreign economic relations--Pakistan. Notes:

Includes bibliographical references (page 102).

Public services and international trade liberalization: human rights and gender implications LCCN: 2012038447 Personal name: Choudhury, Barnali 1974- Main title: Public services and international trade liberalization: human rights and gender implications/Barnali Choudhury. Published/Created: Cambridge [UK]; New York: Cambridge University Press 2012. Description: xvi, 362 p.; 24 cm. Links: Cover image http://assets.cambridge.org/97811070/26568/cover/9781107026568.jpg ISBN: 9781107026568 (hardback) LC classification: K3973 .C48 2012 Summary: "Does public service liberalization pose a threat to gender and human rights? Traditionally considered essential services provided by a state to its citizens, public services are often viewed as public goods which embody social values. Subjecting them to market ideology thus raises concerns that the intrinsic social nature of these services will be negated. Moreover, as those most likely to be reliant on public services, public service liberalization may also further marginalize women. Nevertheless, states continue to increasingly liberalize public services. Barnali Choudhury explores the implications of public service liberalization. Using primarily a legal approach, but drawing from case studies, empirical research and gender theories, she examines whether liberalization under the General Agreement on Trade in Services and other liberalization vehicles such as preferential trade and investment agreements compromise human rights and gender objectives"-- Provided by publisher. "Does public service liberalization pose a threat to gender and human rights? Traditionally considered essential services provided by a state to its citizens, public services are often viewed as public goods which embody social values. Subjecting them to market ideology thus raises concerns that the intrinsic social nature of these services will be negated. Moreover, public service liberalization may also further marginalize women, as those most likely to be reliant on public services. Nevertheless, states continue to increasingly liberalize public services"-- Provided by publisher. Contents: Machine generated contents note: Introduction; Part I. Foundations: 1. International economic law and human rights; 2. Public services; 3. Instruments for liberalizing public services; Part II. Human Rights and Gendered Implications of Liberalization of Public Services: 4. Liberalization of water services; 5. Liberalization of educational services; 6. Liberalization of health services; 7. Accounting for the differential implications of liberalized public services on developing countries and women; Part III. The Future of Liberalization of Public Services: 8. Should public services continue to be liberalized?; 10. Conclusion. Subjects: General Agreement on Trade in Services (Organization) Vienna Convention on the Law of Treaties (1969) Service industries--Law and legislation. Investments, Foreign--Law and legislation. Human rights. Women's rights. LAW/International. Notes: Includes index. Series: Cambridge international trade and economic law

Regional integration and trade in Africa LCCN: 2014028329 Main title: Regional integration and trade in Africa/edited by Mthuli Ncube, Senior Research Fellow, Blavatrik School of Government, University of Oxford (on leave from the African Development Bank), Issa Faye, Manager of the Research Division, African Development Bank, Audrey Verdier-Chouchane, Chief Research Economist, African Development Bank. Published/Produced: Houndmills, Basingstoke, Hampshire: Palgrave Macmillan 2015. Description: xxiii 238 pages; 23 cm Links: Cover image http://www.netread.com/jcusers2/bk1388/046/9781137462046/image/lgcover.9781137462046.jpg ISBN: 9781137462046 (hardback) LC classification: HF1611 .R437 2015 Related names: Ncube, Mthuli 1963- Faye, Issa 1972- Verdier-Chouchane, Audrey 1973- Summary: “Regional integration has been adopted by many African governments as a response to difficulties facing national markets in landlocked countries. However, despite the aspiring targets they have experienced setbacks due to poor implementation. This book reviews the current trends, challenges and potential benefits of regional integration and trade in Africa, in a context of rising interest and momentum among African leaders on the topic.This study explores the many facets of regional trade, its implementation gaps and positive effects through empirical studies covering various African sub-regions and using different theoretical approaches. It analyses trade performance against full potential, its mitigated impact on the competitiveness, industrialization and economic diversification of African countries as well as the much debated effect of monetary unions on regional trade in the region. It provides valuable policy recommendations aimed at stimulating the debate among the government, private sector and development community on the ways to promote regional trade for Africa's economic development.Regional Integration and Trade in Africa examines various aspects of regional integration and trade in Africa, and will be of interest to scholars, students, researchers, policy-makers, and professionals"-- Provided by publisher. Contents: Machine generated contents note: -- Overview Chapter: Understanding Africa's Regional Trade; Mthuli Nucbe, Issa Faye and Audrey Verdier-Chouchane Part I: Intra-African Trade Performance and Regional Integration 1. Competitiveness and Integration through Trade in CEMAC Countries: Comparative Advantage and Contribution to the Trade Balance; Jospeh Parfait Owoundi 2. Economic integration, Trade Facilitation and Agricultural Exports Performance in ECOWAS Sub-Region; Wumi Olayiwola, Evans Osabuohien, Henry Okodua and Oluyomi Ola-David 3. The Impact of Trade Liberalization on Export Growth and Import Growth in Sub-Saharan Africa; Lanre Kassim Part II: Measuring Trade Potential: The Gravity Model Approach 4. Market Integration in the ECCAS Sub-Region; De;sire; Avom and Mouhamed Mbouandi Njikam 5. Regional Integration and Trade in Sub-Saharan Africa 1993-2010: An Augmented Gravity Model; Edris Seid Part III: Industrialization Strategy And The Issue Of Deindustrialization 6. Malawi's Trade Policies, Market Structure, and Manufacturing Performance 1967-2002; Hopestone Kayiska Chavula 7. Impact of South-South and North-South Trade on Industrialization in Africa; Henri Atangana Ondoa and Tabi Henri Ngoa Part IV: Impact of Currency Union on Trade 8. Impact of Monetary Unions on Trade: The Case of WAEMU; Ibrahima Camara 9. Trade Agreements and Flows in ECOWAS: Is a Single Currency the Determining Factor?; Benjamin Ndong and Sokhana Diarra Mboup 10. A DSGE Model of Trade and Risk-sharing

Effects of Currency Union on Economic Integration of the CFA Zone; Thierry Kame BabillaConcluding Chapter: Enhancing Intra-African Trade through Regional Integration; Mthuli Ncube, Issa Faye and Audrey Verdier-Chouchane. Subjects: Business & Economics/Development/Economic Development. Business & Economics/Economics/General. Africa--Commercial policy. Africa--Commerce. Africa--Economic integration. Africa--Foreign economic relations.

The effect of trade liberalization on Myanmar foreign trade with selected Asian countries LCCN: 2014315200 Personal name: Minn Maung Oo, author. Main title: The effect of trade liberalization on Myanmar foreign trade with selected Asian countries/Minn Maung Oo. Published/Produced: Khon Kaen, Thailand: Mekong Institute, [2013] Description: ix, 34 pages; 29 cm Related names: Mekong Institute, issuing body. Notes: "December 2013." Includes bibliographical references (pages 31-32). In English. Series: Mekong Institute research working paper series 2013; paper no. 8/2013

The Oxford handbook on the World Trade Organization LCCN: 2012002801 Main title: The Oxford handbook on the World Trade Organization/edited by Amrita Narlikar, Martin Daunton and Robert M. Stern. Published/Created: New York: Oxford University Press, USA 2012. Description: xxvii, 849 p.; 26 cm. ISBN: 9780199586103 (hardback) LC classification: HF1385 .O94 2012 Related names: Narlikar, Amrita. Daunton, M. J. (Martin J.) Stern, Robert M. (Robert Mitchell) 1927- Summary: "The Oxford Handbook on the World Trade Organization provides an authoritative and cutting-edge account of the World Trade Organization. Its purpose is to provide a holistic understanding of what the WTO does, how it goes about fulfilling its tasks, its achievements and problems, and how it might contend with some critical challenges. The Handbook benefits from an interdisciplinary approach. The editorial team comprises a transatlantic partnership between a political scientist, a historian, and an economist. The distinguished and international team of contributors to the volume includes leading political scientists, historians, economists, lawyers, and practitioners working in the area of multilateral trade. All the chapters present original and state-of-the-art research material. They critically engage with existing academic and policy debates, and also contribute to the evolution of the field by setting the agenda for current and future WTO studies.The Handbook is aimed at research institutions, university academics, post-graduate students, and final-year undergraduates working in the areas of international organization, trade policy and negotiations, global economic governance, and economic diplomacy. As such, it should find an enthusiastic readership amongst students and scholars in History, Economics, Political Science, International Relations, Public Policy, and Law. Equally important, the book should have direct relevance for diplomats, international bureaucrats, government officials, and other policy-makers and practitioners in the area of trade and economic governance"-- Provided by publisher. "Short Description The Oxford Handbook on the World Trade Organization provides an authoritative and cutting-edge account of the World Trade Organization - what it does, how it goes about fulfilling its tasks, its achievements and problems, and how it might contend with some critical challenges"-- Provided by publisher. Contents: Machine generated contents note: -- Introduction, Amrita Narlikar, Martin Daunton, and Robert M. Stern -- Part I: Theory of Multilateral Trade Liberalization -- 1. The Case for a Multilateral Trade Organization, Robert E. Baldwin -- 2. The Inconsistent Quartet: Free Trade Versus Competing Goals, Martin Daunton -- 3. Trade Liberalization and Domestic Politics, Judith Goldstein -- Part II: Institutional Evolution: Building up the World Trade Organization -- 4. International Trade Organization, Richard Toye -- 5. The expanding mandate of the GATT: The First Seven Rounds, Thomas Zeiler -- 6. Uruguay Round Negotiations and the Creation of the WTO, Ernest Preeg -- Part III: The Process Behind the Workings of the WTO -- 7. The Role of the Director-General and the Secretariat, Richard Blackhurst -- 8. Defining the Borders of the WTO Agenda, Marion Jansen -- 9. Collective Agency, Systemic Consequences: Bargaining Coalitions in the WTO, Amrita Narlikar -- Part IV: Agency in the WTO -- 10. The Influence of the EU in the World Trade System, Patrick Messerlin -- 11. The Role of the US: A Multi-level explanation for Decreased Support over Time, Todd Allee -- 12. The Role of the B(R)ICS: System supporters or Change agents in the WTO?, Brendan Vickers -- 13. Least Developed Countries: Growing Voice, Shishir Priyadarshi and Taufiqur Rahman -- 14. Awkward Partners: NGOs and Social Movements in the WTO, Jens Steffek -- 15. What happened to the Influence of Business? Corporations and Organised Labour in the WTO, Steven McGuire -- Part V: The Substance of the Agreements -- 16. Trade in Manufactures and Agricultural Products: The Dangerous Link? (Helen Coskeran, Dan Kim, Amrita Narlikar) -- 17. Trade in Services in the WTO: From Marrakech (1994) to Doha (2001) to..., Rudolf Adlung -- 18. Trade Related Intellectual Property Rights (TRIPs), Keith Maskus -- 19. Rules: Anti-dumping, Countervailing Duties, and Safeguards, Michael Finger -- 20. Regulatory Measures: SPS, TBT, Customs Valuation, Robert Howse -- Part VI: Implementation and Enforcement -- 21. Trade Policy Review Mechanism, Sam Laird and Raymundo Valdes -- 22. Dispute Settlement Mechanism - Analysis and Problems, Manfred Elsig, Joost Pauwelyn and Thoms Bernhauer -- 23. DSM - The Appellate Body - Assessment and Problems, Mitsuo Matsushita -- 24. Interpretation and Institutional Choice at the WTO, Gregory Shaffer and Joel Trachtman -- 25. The DSM: Ensuring Compliance?, Alan O. Sykes -- Part VII: Challenges to the System -- 26. Persistent Deadlock at Doha, Cedric Dupont and Manfred Elsig -- 27. The Role of Domestic Courts in the Implementation of WTO Law: The Political Economy of Separation of Powers and Checks and Balances, Thomas Cottier -- 28. Preferential Trading Arrangements, Richard Baldwin -- 29. New Issues in Food, Agriculture, and Natural Resources, Tim Josling -- Part VIII: Ethical Issues -- 30. Fairness in the WTO Trading System, Andrew G. Brown and Robert M. Stern -- 31. Labour Standards and Human Rights, Drusilla Brown -- 32. Trade and the Environment, Meera Fickling and Gary Hufbauer -- Part IX: Reform of the WTO and Global Economic Governance -- 33. Proposals for Reform: A Synthesis and Assessment, Bernard Hoekman -- 34. The WTO and Institutional (In)Coherence, Steven Bernstein and Erin Hannah. Subjects: World Trade Organization--Handbooks, manuals, etc. International trade--Handbooks, manuals, etc. Political Science/International Relations/Trade & Tariffs. Business & Economics/ Accounting/Governmental. Notes: Includes bibliographical references and index.

The readiness of MSMEs in facing ASEAN economic community 2015 LCCN: 2014031864 Main title: The readiness of MSMEs in facing ASEAN economic community 2015/editor, Tulus Tahi Hamonangan Tambunan, Phd. Published/Produced: Hauppauge, New York: Nova Science Publishers, Inc., [2014] Description: x 228 pages: illustration: 25 cm ISBN: 9781633210295 (hardcover) LC classification: HD2346.A75 R43 2014 Related names: Tambunan, Tulus 1956- Contents: Introduction -- Development and constraints -- ASEAN economic community 2015: trade liberalization -- ASEAN economic community 2015: investment liberalization -- Access to trade facilitation -- Integration into e-trade -- The use of B2B providers in international trade. Subjects: Small business--Southeast Asia. Economic development--Southeast Asia. Southeast Asia--Commerce. Notes: Includes index. Series: Economic issues, problems and perspectives

The trade policy of emerging powers: strategic choices of Brazil and India LCCN: 2013031375 Personal name: Mahrenbach, Laura Carsten 1982- Main title: The trade policy of emerging powers: strategic choices of Brazil and India/Laura Carsten Mahrenbach, Post-doctoral Fellow, Technische Universität Dresden, Germany. Published/Produced: Basingstoke, Hampshire: Palgrave Macmillan 2013. Description: xii 245 pages; 23 cm. ISBN: 9781137303707 (hardback) LC classification: HF1413 .M294 2013 Summary: “As emerging powers deepen their involvement in world trade and global governance, it is crucial to explore the what and the why of their strategic choices vis-a-vis the World Trade Organization. This book does just that, examining the trade policy decisions of two emerging power states, Brazil and India, since 2001. In this timely work, Laura Carsten Mahrenbach develops a broad-based analytical framework which addresses trade policy within EP states, in their regions and on the global level. The findings underline the importance of examining domestic factors when trying to understand strategic decisions by emerging powers. They also have important implications for our understanding of the role of emerging power states in global (trade) governance"-- Provided by publisher. Contents: Machine generated contents note: -- 1. Empirical Puzzle, Arguments and Research Design -- 2. Brazil: Context and Trade Liberalization -- 3. Brazil: Dispute Settlement and Conclusions -- 4. India: Context and Trade Liberalization -- 5. India: Dispute Settlement and Conclusions -- 6. Conclusions, Revised Framework and Implications. Subjects: Business & Economics/Development/Economic Development. Political Science/International Relations/Trade & Tariffs. Social Science/Developing Countries. Developing countries--Commercial policy. Developing countries--Foreign economic relations. Brazil--Commerce. India--Commerce. Notes: Includes bibliographical references (pages 218-236) and index. Series: International political economy series

The United States, Japan, and free trade: moving in the same direction? LCCN: 2012006001 Main title: The United States, Japan, and free trade: moving in the same direction?/Julia F. Lowell ... [et al.]. Published/ Created: Santa Monica, CA: RAND, c2012. Description: xiv, 41 p.; 28 cm. ISBN: 9780833060402 (pbk.: alk. paper) 0833060406 (pbk.: alk. paper) LC classification: HF1456.5.P3 U55 2012 Related names: Lowell, Julia 1961- Kokusai Kōryū Kikin. Nichi-Bei Sentā. Center for Asia-Pacific Policy (Rand Corporation) Contents: Preface -- Tables -- Summary -- Acknowledgments -- Abbreviations -- Introduction -- The Trans-Pacific Partnership -- The effects of trade liberalization -- The U.S. economic policy environment -- The U.S. political environment -- The Japanese economic policy environment -- The Japanese political environment -- Assessing trade policy options -- Conclusion -- Bibliography. Subjects: United States--Foreign economic relations--Pacific Area. Pacific Area--Foreign economic relations--United States. Japan--Foreign economic relations--Pacific Area. Pacific Area--Foreign economic relations--Japan. United States--

Commercial policy. Japan-- Commercial policy. Notes: "Sponsored by the Japan Foundation Center for Global Partnership." "Center for Asia Pacific Policy; International Programs at RAND." Includes bibliographical references (p. 37-41). Series: Occasional paper; OP-363-CGP Occasional paper (Rand Corporation); OP-363-CGP.

The WTO and trade in services LCCN: 2011942534 Main title: The WTO and trade in services/edited by Bernard Hoekman. Published/Created: Cheltenham, UK; Northampton, MA, USA: Edward Elgar, c2012. Description: 2 v.: ill.; 25 cm. Links: Table of contents only http://www.loc.gov/catdir/toc/fy13pdf01/2011942534.html ISBN: 9781843762607 (2 v. set) 1843762609 (2 v. set) LC classification: K3973 .W758 2012 Variant title: World Trade Organization and trade in services Related names: Hoekman, Bernard M. 1959- Contents: Vol. 1: The role of services in the structure of production and trade: stylized facts from a cross-country analysis/Joseph F. Francois and Kenneth A. Reinert -- The structure of services in Europe: a conceptual framework/André Sapir -- Producer services, scale, and the division of labor/Joseph F. Francois -- Principles in trade in services/Richard H. Snape -- Principles in factor-related trade in services/Brian Hindley -- Comparative advantage and international trade and investment in services/Alan V. Deardorff -- The muddles over outsourcing/Jagdish Bhagwati, Arvind Panagariya and T.N. Srinivasan -- Service multinationals: conceptualization, measurement and theory/J.J. Boddewyn, Marsha Baldwin Halbrich and A.C. Perry -- Modeling the offshoring of white-collar services: from comparative advantage to the new theories of trade and foreign direct investment/James R. Markusen -- Measurement and classification of service sector activity: data needs for GATS 2000/Obie G. Whichard -- Measuring U.S. international goods and services transactions/Robert E. Baldwin and Fukunari Kimura -- Productivity in the services sector/Jack E. Triplett and Barry P. Bosworth -- The EU-US total factor productivity gap: an industry perspective/Karel Havik, Kieran Mc Morrow, Werner Röger and Alessandro Turrini -- Measuring impediments to trade in services/Tony Warren and

Christopher Findlay -- Measuring the cost of barriers to trade in services/Philippa Dee, Kevin Hanslow and Tien Phamduc -- Tradable services: understanding the scope and impact of services offshoring/J. Bradford Jensen and Lori G. Kletzer -- Quantifying the impact of services liberalization in a developing country/Denise Eby Konan and Keith E. Maskus -- The impact on Russia of WTO accession and the DDA: the importance of liberalization of barriers against FDI in services for growth and poverty reduction/Thomas Rutherford, David Tarr and Oleksandr Shepotylo -- The effects of the Services Directive on intra-EU trade and FDI/Henk Kox and Arjan Lejour -- Services policy reform and economic growth in transition economies/Felix Eschenbach and Bernard Hoekman -- International provision of trade services, trade, and fragmentation/Alan V. Deardorff -- Transportation costs and international trade in the second era of globalization/David Hummels -- Markct structure, trade liberalization and the GATS/Joseph Francois and Ian Wooton -- Liberalization of trade in services in developing countries/James Hodge -- How does foreign entry affect domestic banking markets?/Stijn Claessens, Asli Demirgüç-Kunt and Harry Huizinga -- Trade in international transport services: the role of competition/Joseph F. Francois and Ian Wooton -- Trade in international maritime services: how much does policy matter?/Carsten Fink, Aaditya Mattoo and Ileana Cristina Neagu -- Some policy lessons from the opening of the Korean insurance market/Yoon Je Cho -- Relaxing the restrictions on the temporary movement of natural persons: a simulation analysis/Terrie L. Walmsley and L. Alan Winters. Vol. 2: Ideas, interests, and institutionalization: "Trade in services" and the Uruguay Round/William J. Drake and Kalypso Nicolaïdis -- Assessing the General Agreement on Trade in Services/Bernard Hoekman -- Turning hills into mountains? Current commitments under the General Agreement on Trade in Services and prospects for change/Rudolf Adlung and Martin Roy -- Services in Doha: what's on the table?/Batshur Gootiiz and Aaditya Mattoo -- The General Agreement on Trade in Services: doomed to fail? Does it matter?/Bernard Hoekman -- China's accession to the WTO: the services dimension/Aaditya Mattoo -- Services policies in transition economies: on the EU and WTO as commitment mechanisms/Felix Eschenbach and Bernard Hoekman -- Public services and the GATS/Rudolf Adlung -- Strengthening WTO member commitments in energy services: problems and prospects/Peter C. Evans -- Regulatory reform and trade liberalization in accountancy services/Claude Trolliet and John Hegarty -- El mess in TELMEX: a comment on Mexico: measures affecting telecommunications services/Damien J. Neven and Petros C. Mavroidis -- Rien ne va plus? Distinguishing domestic regulation from market access in GATT and GATS/Joost Pauwelyn -- Liberalization of trade in services and trade negotiations/Alejandro Jara and M. del Carmen Domínguez -- Services in a development round: three goals and three proposals/Aaditya Mattoo -- Completing the GATS Framework: safeguards, subsidies and government procurement/Pierre Sauvé -- Regional agreements and trade in services; policy issues/Aaditya Mattoo -- Services liberalization in the new generation of preferential trade agreements (PTAs): how much further than the GATS?/Martin Roy, Juan Marchetti and Hoe Lim -- Services provisions in regional trade agreements: stumbling blocks or building blocks for multilateral liberalization?/Carsten Fink and Marion Jansen -- Revisiting regional trade agreements and their impact on services trade/Mario Marconini. Subjects: World Trade Organization. Service industries--Law and legislation. Foreign trade regulation. Notes: "An Elgar research collection." Includes bibliographical references. Series: Critical perspectives on the global trading system and the WTO; 20 Critical perspectives on the global trading system and the WTO; 20.

Trade in Asia LCCN: 2014959491 Main title: Trade in Asia/edited by Richard Pomfret. Published/Produced: Cheltenham, UK; Northampton, MA, USA: Edward Elgar Publishing, [2015] Description: xxv, 664 pages: illustrations; 25 cm. ISBN: 9781783479481 1783479485 Related names: Pomfret, Richard W. T., editor. Contents: Introduction/Richard Pomfret -- Part I: Flying geese and NIEs -- A theory of unbalanced growth in the world economy/Kaname Akamatsu -- The "flying geese" model of Asian economic development: origin, theoretical extensions, and regional policy implications/Kiyoshi Kojima --

Economic development in East Asia: doing what comes naturally?/James Riedel -- Part II: The second generation -- Can the East Asian model of development be generalized?/William R. Cline -- Can the East Asian model of development be generalized? A comment/Gustav Ranis -- Overview: the making of a miracle/World Bank -- Part III: The benefits of openness -- Trade liberalization, intermediate inputs, and productivity: evidence from Indonesia/Mary Amiti and Jozef Konings -- Productivity and turnover in the export market: micro-level evidence from the Republic of Korea and Taiwan (China)/Bee Yan Aw, Sukkyun Chung and Mark J. Roberts -- Part IV: Subcontracting and other institutional novelties -- Manufactured exports from less-developed countries and multinational firms/G.K. Helleiner -- International trade and industrial upgrading in the apparel commodity chain/Gary Gereffi -- Part V: Subregional zones -- Subregional economic zones: a new motive force in Asia-Pacific development/Chia Siow Yue and Lee Tsao Yuan -- Sub-regional economic zones/Richard Pomfret -- Sub-regional cooperation and developmental regionalism: the case of BIMP- AGA/Christopher M. Dent and Peter Richter -- Part VI: Regional integration -- The East Asian trading bloc: an analytical history/Peter A. Petri -- Open regionalism: the nature of Asia Pacific integration/Peter Drysdale, Andrew Elek and Hadi Soesastro -- Is SAARC a viable economic block? Evidence from gravity model/M. Kabir Hassan -- Bilateral trade agreements/Jayant Menon -- Regionalism in the Asia-Pacific region: how wide, how deep?/Richard Pomfret -- East Asian regionalism: much ado about nothing?/John Ravenhill -- Part VII: ASEAN -- A new look at Intra-ASEAN economic co-operation/Mari Pangestu, Hadi Soesastro and Mubariq Ahmad -- Clothes without an emperor: analysis of the preferential tariffs in ASEAN/Miriam Manchin and Annette O. Pelkmans-Balaoing -- ASEAN economic community: a general equilibrium analysis/Peter A. Petri, Michael G. Plummer and Fan Zhai -- Part VIII: RVCs and GVCs -- China's emergence and the reorganisation of trade flows in Asia/Guillaume Gaulier, Françoise Lemoine and Deniz Onal-Kesenci -- Singapore and ASEAN in the new regional division of labor/Prema-chandra Athukorala -- Production networks and trade patterns in East Asia: regionalization or globalization?/Prema-chandra Athukorala. Subjects: Asia--Commerce. Notes: Includes bibliographical references. Series: The international library of critical writings in economics; 301 An Elgar reference collection International library of critical writings in economics; 301. Elgar reference collection.

Trade liberalization, investment and economic integration in African regional economic communities towards the African common market LCCN: 2012449449 Main title: Trade liberalization, investment and economic integration in African regional economic communities towards the African common market/United Nations Conference on Trade and Development, UNCTAD [and] African Union. Published/Created: Geneva: United Nations 2012. Description: xiv, 61 p.: col. ill., col. Map; 30 cm. Links: http://archive.unctad.org/en/docs/ditctncd2011d2_en.pdf ISBN: 9789211128444 9211128447 LC classification: HF2416 .T73 2012 Related names: United Nations Conference on Trade and Development. African Union. Subjects: Free trade--Africa. Investments--Africa. International economic integration. Economic development--Africa. Africa--Economic integration. Notes: "UNCTAD/DITC/TNCD/2011/2"--T.p. verso. "United Nations publication sales no.: E.12.II.D.4"--T.p. verso. "This report was prepared by UNCTAD and the African Union (AU) Commission at the request of the latter"--P. x. Includes bibliographical references.

Trade liberalization, product variety and growth. LCCN: 2014360564 Main title: Trade liberalization, product variety and growth. Published/Produced: Mumbai: Export-Import Bank of India 2014. Description: 96 pages

Trade policy in Asia: higher education and media services LCCN: 2014005225 Main title: Trade policy in Asia: higher education and media services/[edited by] Christopher Findlay (University of Adelaide, Australia), Hildegunn Kyvik Nordas (Organisation for Economic Co-operation and Development, France) Gloria Pasadilla (APEC Secretariat, Singapore). Published/Produced: New Jersey: World Scientific, [2014] Description: x, 413 pages; 24 cm. ISBN: 9789814590198 (hardcover: alk. paper) LC classification: LC67.68.A78 T73

2014 Related names: Findlay, Christopher C. (Christopher Charles), editor of compilation. Nordås, Hildegunn Kyvik, editor of compilation. Pasadilla, Gloria, editor of compilation. Vincent-Lancrin, Stéphan. From cross-border higher education to trade in education services. Contains (work): Summary: "Education and media services have much in common. Both provide services that embody local cultures, in which there is extensive public sector participation and significant domestic regulation. Both are dramatically affected by the information and communications technology revolution. The production of information content now involves huge costs in terms of research and development or artistic talent, whilst the cost of making such products available to other consumers is very low. This in turn challenges the effectiveness of domestic regulation and raises fundamental questions about its purpose, calling for an increased scope for international trade and investment, and the development of supply chains. Yet, both areas are lightly committed in international trade agreements like the GATS. Trade Policy in Asia responds to these issues to provide readers with a comprehensive, consistent treatment of policy in the higher education and media services sector across various Asian economies. It identifies commonalities across these sectors and highlights critical trade policy implications. Education services themes include growth and impediments involved in trade and investment; the emergence of a 'new wave' of globalization; obstacles faced by domestic providers in supplying services; a common ambition to become an education services hub for international students; and the scope for greater international cooperation in research. Media services themes include the impact of new technology on content delivery options and associated problems for policy implementation and copyright protection, and the new challenges of globalization for social goals relating to local cultures, as well as risks involved in implementing related policies"-- Provided by publisher. Contents: From cross-border higher education to trade in education services/Stéphan Vincent-Lancrin -- People's Republic of China's regulations in higher education services/Xingde Zhu -- Trade and investment in higher education services in Hong Kong, China/Jane Drake-Brockman --

International transactions in tertiary education services: the case of Japan/Shintaro Hamanaka -- Trade liberalization and domestic regulations: implications for Malaysia as a regional education hub/Siew Yean Tham -- Internationalization of tertiary education services in Singapore/Mun-Heng Toh -- Audiovisual services: international trade and cultural policy/Gillian Doyle -- Audiovisual services in India/Arpita Mukherjee -- Audiovisual services in the Republic of Korea: market development and policies/Yeongkwan Song. Subjects: Education, Higher--Economic aspects--Asia. Transnational education--Economic aspects--Asia. Mass media--Economic aspects--Asia. Asia--Commercial policy. Notes: Includes bibliographical references and index. Series: World Scientific studies in international economics; vol. 36

Zimbabwe's experience with trade liberalization LCCN: 2013441415 Personal name: Makochekanwa, Albert, author. Main title: Zimbabwe's experience with trade liberalization/by Makochekanwa Albert, Hurungo T. James, and Kambarami Prosper. Published/Produced: Nairobi: African Economic Research Consortium 2012. Description: 36 pages: illustrations; 25 cm. ISBN: 9789966023179 9966023178 LC classification: HF2442 .M35 2012 Related names: Hurungo, James, author. Kambarami, Prosper, author. Subjects: Free trade--Zimbabwe. Zimbabwe--Commercial policy. Notes: "October 2012." Includes bibliographical references (pages 32-33). Series: AERC research paper; 245 AERC research paper; 245.

INDEX

#

A

B

C

D

E

F

J

K

L

M

Q

R

S

T

U

V

W

Y

Z